SpringerBriefs in Education

More information about this series at http://www.springer.com/series/8914

Ramon Flecha (Ed.)
INCLUD-ED Consortium

Successful Educational Actions for Inclusion and Social Cohesion in Europe

 Springer

Ramon Flecha (Ed.)
INCLUD-ED Consortium
University of Barcelona
Barcelona
Spain

ISSN 2211-1921   ISSN 2211-193X (electronic)
ISBN 978-3-319-11175-9   ISBN 978-3-319-11176-6   (eBook)
DOI 10.1007/978-3-319-11176-6

Library of Congress Control Number: 2014948767

Springer Cham Heidelberg New York Dordrecht London

Printed on acid-free paper

Springer is part of Springer Science+Business Media (www.springer.com)

Contents

Contributions to this Publication

Universitat de Barcelona

CREA—Centre of Research in Theories and Practices that Overcome Inequalities, Spain, Barcelona

- Elena Duque
- Ramon Flecha (Main researcher)
- Rocío García
- Paloma García
- Carme García
- Jesús Gómez
- Aitor Gómez
- Antonio Latorre
- Silvia Molina
- Esther Oliver
- Ignasi Puigdellívol
- Lídia Puigvert
- Sandra Racionero
- Gisela Redondo
- Montse Sánchez
- Marta Soler
- Rosa Valls

Donau-Universität Krems—Universität für Weiterbildung

Austria, Krems

- Silvia Benda-Kahri
- Wolfgang Jütte

- Jörg Markowitsch
- Thomas Pfeffer
- Stephanie Rammel
- Lil Reif

Centre for European Policy Studies

Belgium, Brussels

- Sergio Carrera
- Anais Faure Atger
- Florian Geyer
- Elspeth Guild

University of Cyprus

Cyprus, Nicosia

- Miranda Christou
- Maria Eliophotou
- Leonidas Kyriakides

Helsingin yliopisto

Finland, Helsinki

- Juhani Hytönen
- Katriina Kaalikoski
- Tiina Kalliokoski
- Anna-Leena Lastikka
- Reko Niemela
- Mikko Ojala
- Jyrki Reunamo

Eötvös Loránd University

Barczi Gusztav Faculty of Special Needs,
Department of Social Sciences,
Hungary, Budapest

- Csaba Banfalvy

Universita degli Studi di Firenze

Italy, Florence

- Steffen Amling
- Giovanna Campani
- Tiziana Chiapelli
- Olivia Salimbeni

Dublin City University

School of Education Studies, Ireland, Dublin

- Charlote Holland
- John Lalor
- Carmel Mulcahy

Vytauto Didžojo Universitetas

Lithuania, Kaunas

- Edita Butrime
- Estela Dauksiene
- Laimute Kardeliene
- Monika Miliusiene
- Margarita Tereseviciene
- Vidmantas Tutlys
- Vaiva Zuzeviciute

Università ta Malta

Malta, Msida

- Jacqueline Azzopardi
- LauraSue Armeni
- Maria Brown
- Suzanne Gatt
- Formosa Marilyn
- Sandra Scicluna

Baltic Institute of Social Sciences

Latvia, Riga

- Inese Supule
- Iveta Kesane
- Liga Krastina
- Brigita Zepa

Universitatea de Vest din Timisoara

Faculty of Sociology and Psychology, Romania, Timissoara

- Teodor Mircea Alexiu

Andragoški Center Republike Slovenije

Slovenia, Ljubljana

- Angelca Ivancic
- Peter Beltram
- Petra Javrh
- Jasmina Mirceva
- Vida Mohorcic Spolar
- Natalija Vrecer

University of Nottingham

Division of Law and Politics, School of Arts, Communications and Humanities, United Kingdom, Nottingham

- Laura Engel
- John Holford
- Viv Mackay
- Nick Walters
- Thushari Welikala
- Urszula Wolski

Autonomous University of Barcelona

Spain, Barcelona

- Javier Díez
- Ainhoa Flecha
- Iñaki Santa Cruz
- Teresa Sordé

Chapter 1
Introduction: From "Best Practices" to Successful Educational Actions

The aim of the research conducted by the INCLUD-ED project is to achieve both academic success and social cohesion for all children and communities in Europe, regardless of their socioeconomic status and/or ethnic background. The project analyzed the educational actions that lead to social inequality, with a particular focus on the actions that contribute to reducing such inequalities and present evidence of educational success. The research studied the impact of these actions and policies on different aspects of society such as employment, housing, health, and social and political participation. On the basis of such research, this chapter distinguishes between actions that obtain excellent results (best practices) and actions that obtain excellent results in many diverse contexts (successful actions). These successful actions are evidence-based solutions that are transferable to different environments and can ground policies.

Many children in Europe are suffering from school failure and early school leaving. These children are at risk of subsequently being excluded from areas such as employment, health, housing, and political participation. European society needs all of these children and youths, their participation and contributions to society throughout their lives. However, to make this possible, we require immediate solutions. This is the reason why *INCLUD-ED: Strategies for inclusion and social cohesion in Europe from education* (2006–2011) was designed, and why children and youths in the most need have been the inspiration for the work conducted by the consortium throughout the project.

In the contemporary knowledge society, education can serve as a powerful resource for achieving the European goal of social cohesion. However, at present, most school systems are failing; many European citizens and their communities are being excluded, both educationally and socially, from the benefits that should be available to all. This situation can be reversed, and recent studies are providing key elements for schools to inform this process. As in medicine, where only treatments that have been proven effective in curing a particular disease are implemented, there is a need to identify those educational and social actions that research shows to be already reversing social and educational exclusion. In the past, educational and

© The Author(s) 2015
R. Flecha (Ed.), INCLUD-ED Consortium, *Successful Educational Actions for Inclusion and Social Cohesion in Europe*, SpringerBriefs in Education,
DOI 10.1007/978-3-319-11176-6_1

social policies have tended to be based on assumptions instead of scientific evidence, leading to the perpetuation of inequalities. However, it is now time for research to collect evidence of success and make it available to policy-makers and society as a whole to inform effective measures and policies that truly address social exclusion.

The aim of *INCLUD-ED: Strategies for inclusion and social cohesion in Europe from education* (2006–2011) is to analyze educational actions that contribute to social cohesion and those that lead to social exclusion in the context of the contemporary European knowledge-based society (Fig. 1.1). INCLUD-ED has striven to clarify successful and unsuccessful strategies in terms of educational success and social inclusion and then use this information to provide key elements and approaches to improve educational and social policy.

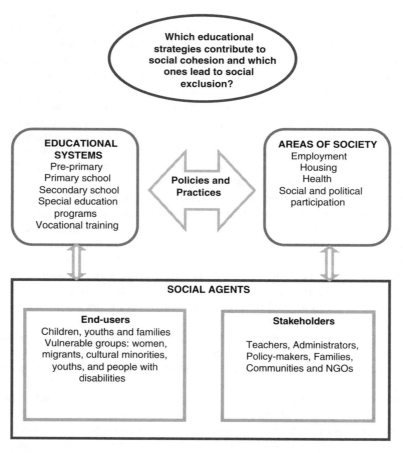

Fig. 1.1 Objectives of the INCLUD-ED project and dimensions of study

The project has identified the elements that can influence school failure or success and their relationship with other areas of society, namely, housing, health, employment, and social and political participation. A specific focus has been placed on social groups that are vulnerable to social exclusion: youths, migrants, cultural minorities, e.g., Roma, women, and persons with disabilities. This all was achieved through the project's efforts to address the following specific objectives:

(1) To analyze the characteristics of the school systems and educational reforms generating low rates of educational and social exclusion and the characteristics of those generating high rates.
(2) To analyze the components of educational practices that are decreasing the rates of school failure and the components of the practices that are increasing such rates.
(3) To study how educational exclusion affects diverse aspects of society (i.e., employment, housing, health, and political participation) and what types of educational provisions contribute to overcoming it.
(4) To investigate how educational exclusion affects diverse sectors of society, particularly the most vulnerable groups (i.e., women, youths, migrants, cultural minorities, and persons with disabilities) and what types of educational provisions contribute to overcoming the discrimination they face.
(5) To analyze the interventions that combine educational policy with other areas of social policies and identify which of them are contributing to overcoming social exclusion and developing social cohesion in Europe.
(6) To study communities involved in learning projects that have developed integrated social and educational interventions that contribute to reducing inequality and marginalization and foster social inclusion and empowerment.

To fulfill these objectives, the work of INCLUD-ED took the form of six projects, grouped into three clusters. Each cluster focused on a specific topic: the first analyzed educational practices and systems, the second explored the connections between education and other areas of social policy, and the third investigated the relationships between schools and communities in greater detail.

INCLUD-ED is the only research project on social sciences highlighted by the European Commission among the 10 success stories of the European Commission's Framework Programmes of Research (European Commission 2011a, b). Its development included 15 European research institutions from throughout the EU.

Throughout the entire research process, INCLUD-ED was not interested in identifying "best practices", which despite their potential to achieve excellent results, are limited to particular contexts. On the contrary, INCLUD-ED was interested in identifying Successful Educational Actions (SEAs), that is, actions that can improve school success and contribute to social cohesion in every context where they are implemented. These actions share characteristics that have been identified in diverse contexts in different countries across Europe—through 20 case studies of effective educational practices and 6 longitudinal case studies of communities involved in learning projects—and which have demonstrated to achieve excellent results.

Successful Educational Actions are effective regardless of the context and therefore are transferrable to other schools and communities to improve school success and social cohesion. Conversely, the concept of "best practices" supports a contextualist perspective that denies the possibility of generalizing successful solutions to educational and social problems. Innovations based on the "best practices" approach do not resort to previous scientific evidence. They are primarily based on assumptions and good intentions that are used to "make something different" to solve a particular social or educational problem. However, those interventions do not rely on comparable evidence regarding whether the same or similar actions have previously realized improvements for similar problems in another instance.

Educational and social initiatives are more effective when they are based on evidence. This is a primary explanation for the success of SEAs: they are transferred to other contexts once they have proven effective. When this does not occur, "best practices" often do not achieve the expected results, and the failure is then explained by the challenging context in which they were implemented. As a consequence, vulnerable children and youths at risk of school failure as well as marginalized communities are denied any expectation of improvement, despite the efforts and resources invested. INCLUD-ED has demonstrated that school failure and social exclusion are not explained by the social characteristics of the context, but by the actions implemented.

Successful Educational Actions, as effective and transferable evidence-based solutions, are the optimal ground for developing educational theory, actual practice and policy making. In this regard, the impact of the INCLUD-ED project on policy development is already reflected in five recommendations that aim to guide improvements in education at the European level, which reflect some of the research outcomes of INCLUD-ED. These recommendations are: the Council conclusions of 11 May 2010 on the social dimension of education and training (2010/C 135/02), a Communication from the EC (January 2011). Tackling early school leaving: A key contribution to the Europe 2020 Agenda, Council Recommendation on policies to reduce early school leaving (June 2011) (10544/11), the European Parliament resolution of 2 April 2009 on educating the children of migrants (2008/2328(INI)), and the European Parliament resolution of 9 March 2011 on the EU strategy on Roma inclusion (2010/2276(INI)).

The scientific impact of INCLUD-ED is demonstrated by its presence in different scientific forums. The major findings have been published in relevant international and national scientific journals,[1] including journals in ISI Journal Citation Reports (JCR), such as the *Journal of Psychodidactics, Signos, European Journal of Education* and *Qualitative Inquiry*. Additionally, INCLUD-ED's findings have been presented, and well received, at the most important international scientific conferences in the fields of education and sociology, including the

---

[1] Some of the evidence presented in this book has already been published in scientific articles in journals such as those mentioned above.

European Conference on Educational Research, the Annual meeting of the American Educational Research Association, the World Educational Research Association, the International Sociological Association World Congress, the European Sociological Association Conference, and the International Congress of Qualitative Inquiry, among others. Moreover, governments, foundations, universities and organizations have invited INCLUD-ED researchers to share the project's results at thematic conferences and institutional events. Selected examples include the ministries of Education of Serbia, Spain, Cyprus and Malta, the DG Research of the European Commission, the European Training Foundation (ETF) and the Organisation for Security and Cooperation in Europe (OSCE). The scientific significance of the INCLUD-ED findings led to its recognition as one of the ten examples of success stories from the European Commission's Framework Programmes of Research. Out of the ten selected projects, INCLUD-ED was the only one in social sciences.[2]

The project has succeeded in achieving social impact by transferring knowledge between researchers, institutions, practitioners and end-users. SEAs have been extended and implemented in variety of national contexts, which led to the support of institutions and local administrations. To do so, the coordinating institution signed several agreements with local administrations, trade unions and universities to make the SEAs accessible to a larger number of individuals who can benefit from the results of the project's research. One example is the agreement between the city council of Albacete (Spain) and CREA-University of Barcelona, which established a collaborative effort to implement the successful actions in two deprived neighborhoods to promote inclusion in several social areas (2009–2013). Another example is the agreement between the University of La Salle (Madrid, Spain) and the University of Barcelona (2010–2012), designed to collaborate on incorporating the findings from INCLUD-ED in the education received by La Salle's students and involve students and professors from La Salle in successful actions implemented in the Madrid area. The third example, the agreement between the University of Kyungnam (South Korea) and the University of Barcelona (2011–2016), involved advice and training on INCLUD-ED's results and their implementation in different areas, the introduction of INCLUD-ED's scientific knowledge and results to improve the training offered at the University of Kyungnam, the involvement of students from the University of Kyungnam as volunteers in successful actions linked with INCLUD-ED and the participation of university professors in activities linked to INCLUD-ED in Korea.

The following chapters present the primary contributions and results from the INCLUD-ED project that generated the aforementioned impacts.

Chapter 2 explains INCLUD-ED's research methodology, the Communicative Methodology, which is based on the premise that knowledge is constructed through

---

[2] This information is available in the *Added value of Research, Innovation and Science portfolio* in the European Commission's Press releases database. MEMO/11/520, at: http://europa.eu/rapid/press-release_MEMO-11-520_en.htm.

dialogues between researchers and end-users, who have not traditionally been allowed to participate in the research process. In this dialogue, the researchers contribute knowledge from the scientific community, which is contrasted with social actors' interpretations from their experiences and common sense. This methodology creates the optimum conditions to achieve the intersubjective relationship necessary for both researchers and social agents to share their knowledge and identify actions that overcome exclusionary elements.

Chapter 3 focuses on three main forms of classroom arrangement: *streaming*, *mixture* and *inclusion*. These three types were clarified by INCLUD-ED according to the ways in which pupils are grouped in schools and human resources are organized. Both *streaming* and *mixture* led to social exclusion, the former because students are separated according to their differences with certain students often receiving additional resources, and the latter because of its failure to account for such differences. Although the European Commission uses the term *streaming* for ability grouping, the more common English literature uses *tracking*, which understandably may be conflated with academic versus technological "tracks" but also involves separation by levels of attainment. In contrast, in an inclusive classroom arrangement, existing human resources are used to improve all pupils' outcomes.

Chapter 4 explains the Successful Educational Actions (SEAs) that achieve both excellent results in terms of academic success and improving social cohesion in schools. Three SEAs are explained: *interactive groups*, *dialogic reading*, and *extended learning time*. These SEAs are in line with the inclusive approach to grouping students and organizing human resources. Concrete data on the pupils' results following the implementation of these SEAs are provided.

Chapter 5 focuses on the Successful Educational Actions that are based on family involvement in schools. The research reveals the connections between certain types of family involvement and pupils' learning outcomes, in relation to the transformation of educational interactions in the school, the street and at the household. Specifically, three Successful Educational Actions involving families will be analyzed: *dialogic literary gatherings*, family involvement in learning activities and their participation in school evaluation and decision-making.

Chapter 6 explains the concept of *schools as learning communities*. Drawing from the results of the INCLUD-ED project's research, the European Commission and the Council of Europe have recommended implementing the transformation of *schools as learning communities* to reduce early school leaving and improve learning outcomes. In schools that function as a *learning community*, teachers, families, pupils, and community members work in close collaboration to implement successful, evidence-based actions in their schools. Currently, there are more than 130 schools, public and private, located in wealthy and low-income areas, with different levels of diversity, and in different countries, that have completed this transformation and are implementing the SEAs and achieving excellent academic and emotional results for their pupils.

Chapter 7 discusses the relationship between education and inclusion/exclusion in other areas of society, namely, employment, health, housing and political participation. Beginning from the literature on this close relationship, particular Integrative Actions that have demonstrated positive results will be described and discussed. The chapter will focus on a case study of a poor neighborhood in which successful actions were implemented through a Dialogic Inclusion Contract that involved the participation of all residents in decision-making.

Finally, Chap. 8 includes recommendations for educational policy development, focusing on the need to invest in evidence-based policies and practices, as a means of improving educational outcomes and reducing costs, which is particularly important in the midst of a worldwide economic recession.

References

Council of the European Union. (2010). Social dimension of education and training (2010/C135/02). Brussels: European Union.

Council of the European Union. (2011). Policies to reduce early school leaving (10544/11). Brussels: European Union.

European Commission. (2011a). Added value of research, innovation and science. MEMO/11/520. Retrieved July 19, from europa.eu/rapid/press-release_MEMO-11-520_en.htm.

European Commission. (2011b). Tackling early school leaving: A key contribution to the Europe 2020 agenda. Brussels: European Commission.

European Parliament. (2009). Educating the children of migrants (2008/2328(INI)). Brussels: European Parliament.

European Parliament. (2011). EU strategy on Roma inclusion (2010/2276(INI)). Brussels: European Parliament.

INCLUD-ED Consortium. (2006–2011). INCLUD-ED Project. Strategies for inclusion and social cohesion in Europe from education, 6th Framework Programme, CIT4-CT-2006-028603. Directorate-General for Research, European Commission.

Chapter 2
The Communicative Methodology of the INCLUD-ED Research

Scientifically published and recognized, the communicative methodology accounts for both the scientific and social aspects of research. In research conducted using the communicative methodology, knowledge is constructed through dialogue between researchers and end-users, who are not traditionally included in the research process. Researchers contribute knowledge from the scientific community, which is contrasted with social actors' interpretations of their life experiences and common sense. This methodology creates the optimal conditions to realize the intersubjective relationship necessary for both researchers and social agents to share their knowledge and identify actions that overcome exclusionary elements. On the basis of this communicative approach, researchers, teachers, parents, pupils and policy-makers have presented the results of INCLUD-ED at the European Parliament with the subsequent approval of resolutions and recommendations by the Parliament, the European Commission and the Council of Europe, all of whom are grounded in the results of the INCLUD-ED project. By overcoming the interpretative hierarchy, the communicative methodology has contributed improving social actors' exclusionary situations.

All of the analyses conducted by INCLUD-ED sought to identify how education can be improved such that all children succeed in school and have greater opportunities for social inclusion. In pursuit of this aim, the perspectives of a wide range of end-users (children, families, and vulnerable groups) and stakeholders (teachers, administrators, policy-makers, communities, and NGOs) were taken into account throughout the research process. Their voices were included in the research design, data collection and analysis, and the dissemination of the results thanks to the use of the Communicative Methodology, which relies on the direct and active participation of the individuals whose experiences are being studied. This involved an on-going dialogue with end-users and stakeholders in the fields of education, culture, and social policy, throughout the 5 years of the project's development. Importantly, the direct involvement of these groups in the research process guaranteed that the research objectives and findings would address the needs of the groups whose

© The Author(s) 2015
R. Flecha (Ed.), INCLUD-ED Consortium, *Successful Educational Actions for Inclusion and Social Cohesion in Europe*, SpringerBriefs in Education,
DOI 10.1007/978-3-319-11176-6_2

experience was being studied and the research results would have a positive impact on their lives by transforming their daily experiences.

The communicative perspective arises from different theoretical contributions. Habermas (1984), in his theory of communicative action, argues that there is no hierarchy between the interpretations of the researcher and the subject and that their relationship should be based on the arguments they provide, not on their social or academic position. The relevance of the subjects' interpretations is considered through the lens of Schütz and Luckmann (1973) phenomenology and it allows the researcher to strengthen the role of typifications in constructing ideal types. However, the communicative perspective also draws on Mead's (1934) symbolic interactionism, which stresses that interactions result in changes in individual interpretations and therefore do not exclusively depend on the individual subject. Garfinkel's (1967) ethnomethodological framework is employed to improve understandings of subjects' insights into their contexts.

The communicative perspective includes the contributions of objectivist and constructivist orientations but emphasizes the processes of critical reflection and self-reflection and intersubjectivity, in which meanings are constructed through communicative interaction among individuals, ultimately leading to agreement. The researcher contributes his or her expertise and knowledge concerning developments in the scientific community to the dialogue, contributions that are subsequently contrasted with the thoughts and experiences of social agents.

The communicative research methodology was analyzed in a book co-authored by Touraine, Wieviorka and Flecha (2004) on the voices of cultural groups in social research. Other renowned authors, such as Jerome Bruner and Amartya Sen, have recognized the scientific and social relevance of this research methodology. In the INCLUD-ED project, we investigated, understood and interpreted educational and social realities using this orientation.

The communicative methodology makes it possible to integrate and incorporate knowledge from different disciplines and orientations, using distinct methods (quantitative and qualitative) and techniques to collect and analyze data; that is, the communicative methodology allows us to apply a mixed methods approach. The different methods were selected according to operational research objectives, but the communicative orientation was maintained throughout the project and applied to all techniques and methods. The communicative methodology seeks to transcend traditional theoretical dualisms in social sciences, such as structure/individual, subject/object, and relativism/universalism and does so by assuming a series of postulates: the universality of language and action, individuals as transformative social agents, communicative rationality, the elimination of the interpretative hierarchy, and dialogic knowledge (Gómez et al. 2011). To apply these principles to an investigation, the methodology requires the researcher to create the conditions that enable intersubjective dialogue between participants and researchers and establish clear criteria and consensus to identify emerging categories and contrast interpretations.

Analyzing the educational strategies that contribute to social cohesion and those that lead to social exclusion requires the inclusion of the most diverse set of voices available (i.e., all related stakeholders and end-users) and the use of a wide range of sources. While the voices of vulnerable groups have traditionally been excluded from research, the communicative methodology relies on the direct and active participation of the individuals whose reality is being studied throughout the research process. After years of doing research "on" them without their involvement, which failed to have any positive effect on their community, the Roma refuse to be involved in any research that applies this exclusionary pattern. Under the communicative methodology, Romani associations have been able to participate in research that takes their voices into account and, as a consequence, provides political and social recommendations that contribute to combating their social exclusion. The INCLUD-ED project relied on the participation of representatives from collectives of immigrants, persons with disabilities, women, youths (at risk) and Roma throughout the entire research process, from the design of the study through the data collection and analysis (Valls and Padrós 2011).

The dialogue is also guaranteed by the creation of consultative mechanisms at key points of the research process. Specifically, we created two consultative bodies: the Advisory Committee (comprising individuals from vulnerable social groups) and the Panel of Experts (which includes renowned experts and scholars in the field and key policy actors). The involvement of their different voices ensures the validity and rigor of the scientific process, thereby contributing to high-quality results. The Advisory Committee (AC) is a consultative body comprising members of the five vulnerable groups studied by INCLUD-ED: women, cultural minorities, migrants, youths, and persons with disabilities. The AC members were selected by all partner institutions based on three criteria: (a) they represented a given vulnerable group and consider themselves at risk of social exclusion as members of that vulnerable group, (b) they did not hold a higher education degree, and (c) they had experience in overcoming inequalities through community participation or social and political involvement. The ten members of the AC had access to the INCLUD-ED results and met with the coordination team to discuss the research. More important, they offered recommendations on how the findings could be applied to have the greatest social and political impact; those recommendations were discussed with the researchers and integrated into the project.

The impact of the Communicative Methodology has already been widely recognized. For example, the Conclusions of the Conference "Science against Poverty", which was held at La Granja, the 8th and 9th of April 2010, stated that the "Critical communicative research perspective has shown to have a significant social and political impact on European educational and social systems" (European Commission 2011).

Consistently adopting this perspective, different research techniques were employed during the 6 projects that comprise the INCLUD-ED project. Those research techniques are qualitative, quantitative and communicative and were used to collect and analyze data to properly achieve the objectives of each of the six projects (Tables 2.1 and 2.2).

While many studies have already described the causes of the educational and social exclusion experienced by vulnerable groups, the focus of INCLUD-ED is not

Table 2.1 Summary of data collection and data analysis techniques employed in INCLUD-ED

	Data collection techniques	Data analysis techniques
Quantitative	Questionnaire	Statistical analysis
	Secondary analysis of existing datasets (e.g., OECD, EUROSTAT, UNESCO, PISA, PIRLS, TIMSS)	
Qualitative	Literature review from main scientific data bases	
	Policy analysis (e.g., Directives, policies, EURYDICE)	
	Documents	Content analysis
	Standardized, open-ended interviews	Communicative data analysis (exclusionary and transformative dimensions)
Communicative	Communicative daily life stories	
	Communicative focus groups	
	Communicative observations	

failure or exclusion but rather to identify actions that are already successfully overcoming the existing barriers that those groups face and that promote their inclusion in different areas of society. For this reason, the communicative data analysis employs a double axis, which involves the exclusionary and transformative dimensions of each category under study. Codifying the data along the exclusionary and transformative dimensions helps us to analyze inequalities, but most importantly, it is effective in identifying solutions through dialogue among all agents involved, that is, the educational strategies that contribute to social cohesion and those that hamper it.

The communicative approach is followed throughout all phases of project development, including the dissemination of the results. The most relevant efforts at communicating our results in terms of policy were the Mid-Term and Final INCLUD-ED Conferences, celebrated at the headquarters of the European Parliament in Brussels in November 2009 and December 2011. Over 300 individuals attended each of the conferences, including members of the European Parliament, representatives of different Member States and regional parliaments, European Commission representatives (DG Research, DG Education, DG Employment, among others), policy-makers, researchers, teachers, family members, citizens, NGOs, companies and children. The audience had the opportunity to hear how Successful Educational Actions (SEAs) are overcoming educational and social exclusion, even in the most disparate neighborhoods in Europe. This entailed a shift from assumptions to the use of evidence in improving education. The development of evidence-based policies was highlighted as being more necessary than ever to overcome the high rates of school failure and early school leaving in Europe.

Table 2.2 Data sources and data collection techniques used in each project

Cluster 1: educational systems in Europe Theories, characteristics and outcomes		
Project 1	*Objective* To analyze the characteristics of the school systems and educational reforms generating low rates of educational and social exclusion and those generating high rates	*Work performed* (a) Literature review on educational reforms and theories to identify the primary debates concerning educational inclusion and exclusion, with a specific focus on vulnerable groups (i.e., cultural minorities, migrants, youths, women, persons with disabilities), the main curricular areas (i.e., math and science, reading and ICT), different levels of education (i.e., pre-primary, primary, secondary) and programs (i.e., vocational training and special education) (b) Policy analysis of educational systems and reforms in 26 EU Member States[a] from the perspective of inclusion and segregation (i.e., orientation, general structure, curriculum) with particular attention being devoted to vulnerable groups (c) Secondary analysis of educational outcomes across Europe using the major international datasets (e.g.,PISA, TIMSS and PIRLS) to analyze early school leaving and school performance
Project 2	*Objective* To analyze the components of educational practices decreasing the rates of school failure and the components of practices that are increasing school failure rates	*Work performed* (a) Literature review on effective educational practices in Europe, focusing on whether they promote inclusion or exclusion and considering three areas of interest: levels of education, areas of knowledge and vulnerable groups (b) Based on the results of Project 1, 20 case studies in 6 different countries (Cyprus, Finland, Hungary, Latvia, Spain and the UK) were conducted on effective educational practices at different educational and programmatic levels. The schools selected fulfilled two criteria: (a) a culturally diverse student body with low socioeconomic status and (b) evidence of progress in academic achievement, relative to other schools in similar contexts. The 20 case studies included: 4 pre-primary schools, 4 primary and 4 secondary schools, 4 vocational training centers, and 4 special education programs in regular schools. Different data collection techniques were employed in each case study: 10 standardized, open-ended interviews (4 students, 3 family members, 3 teachers and other professionals from the school community), 1 communicative focus group with teachers, and 5 communicative observations of effective educational practices

(continued)

Table 2.2 (continued)

Cluster 1: educational systems in Europe

Theories, characteristics and outcomes

Outcomes Cluster 1 allowed the research team to identify the educational actions contributing to improving academic achievement and realizing positive modes of coexistence among diverse social groups regardless of their socially disadvantaged context and membership in vulnerable groups

Cluster 2: connections between educational and social exclusion and inclusion

Structures, social agents, and policies

	Objective	*Work performe*
Project 3	To study how educational exclusion affects diverse aspects of society (i.e., employment, housing, health, political participation) and what types of educational provision contribute to overcoming it	(a) Literature review on the relationship between educational outcomes and exclusion or inclusion in four aspects of society (i.e., employment, housing, health, and social and political participation) and on the actions that allow individuals to overcome these inequalities (b) Secondary analysis of existing datasets on social exclusion indicators (c) Policy analysis on the role of education in the different aspects of society highlighted in EU recommendations and directives (d) Standardized, open-ended interviews (170) with: professionals and policy-makers involved in the different aspects of society studied and working at the national level in different countries (Slovenia, Spain, Italy, Austria, Romania, Belgium and Finland), as well as with professionals and policy-makers working at the European level
	Objective	*Work performed*
Project 4	To investigate how educational exclusion affects diverse sectors of society, particularly the most vulnerable groups, and what forms of educational provision contribute to overcoming the resulting discrimination	(a) Literature review on the ways that vulnerable groups—women, migrants, cultural minorities, youths and persons with disabilities—are affected by educational and social exclusion (b) Survey of NGOs working with vulnerable groups. The survey focused on identifying—from the perspective of social agents—how educational exclusion affects members of the vulnerable groups

(continued)

Table 2.2 (continued)

Cluster 2: connections between educational and social exclusion and inclusion Structures, social agents, and policies	
	studied and what forms of educational provision contribute to overcoming the discrimination that they face (c) Communicative daily life stories (25) and focus groups (10) with members of vulnerable groups to analyze how, from their perspective, educational exclusion affects them and which strategies helped them to overcome the various barriers they face
Project 5	*Objective* To analyze the interventions that combine educational policy and other areas of social policy and identify which of those interventions are effective in overcoming social exclusion and developing social cohesion in Europe	*Work performed* (a) Policy analysis of European directives and policy documents in the different social areas with the aim of identifying the educational components that have contributed to vulnerable groups acquiring rights (strengthening citizenship) (b) Literature review of integrative actions: policies that connect education with other areas of social policy and have achieved significant results in overcoming social exclusion in the areas of health, housing, employment, and participation (c) In-depth analysis of 18 selected integrative actions

Outcomes Cluster 2 detailed how education can promote social inclusion, especially among vulnerable groups, in different areas of society, specifically in employment, health, housing and social and political participation. In particular, the research conducted in this cluster identified the central characteristics of integrative successful actions that can be transferred to and recreated in other contexts

(continued)

Table 2.2 (continued)

| Cluster 3: social cohesion from below |
| Strengthening social cohesion through education |

| Cluster 3: social cohesion from below |
| Strengthening social cohesion through education |

Project	Objective	Work performed
6	To study communities involved in learning projects that have developed integrated social and educational interventions that contribute to reducing inequalities and marginalization and foster social inclusion and empowerment	*Work performed*

Work performed

(a) Four-year, longitudinal case studies of 6 schools (in Malta, the UK, Finland, Lithuania, and Spain), selected according to the following three criteria:

  (1) Schools that have demonstrated their students' academic success (as reflected by their educational attainment) relative to schools with similar characteristics,

  (2) Schools that serve a high percentage of low-SES students and those with minority backgrounds,

  (3) Schools with substantial community involvement. Quantitative and qualitative data collection methods were used, including: a questionnaire administered to families and pupils; communicative life-stories collected from pupils and relatives; open-ended interviews with members of the local administration, NGOs and professionals; focus groups with professionals; and communicative observations of community participation in the school

The following techniques were used in each case study: 13 standardized, open-ended interviews (5 with representatives of the local administration, 5 with representatives of other community organizations involved in the local project, and 3 with professionals working on the local project), 13 communicative daily life stories collected from end-users (6 from family members and 7 from students), 1 communicative focus group with professionals working on the local project, 5 communicative observations, and 2 questionnaires administered to end-users (one addressed to family members and the other addressed to students)

(continued)

Table 2.2 (continued)

Cluster 3: social cohesion from below Strengthening social cohesion through education	(b) Longitudinal case studies and cross-case studies were performed, based on the data collected for each school in the four rounds. For each round, specific research questions were defined to analyze new topics taking into account previously obtained results. The first round focused on educational strategies that lead to social cohesion and improved academic results related to community involvement. The second focused on the different types of family and community participation. The third round focused on the connection between those different types of family and community participation and students' academic and non-academic improvements. The fourth round focused on this connection but concerning the transformation of the neighborhood in terms of the following social areas: housing, health, employment, and social and political participation

Outcomes Cluster 3 shed light on the specific types of family and community participation in schools that contribute to students' academic success and social cohesion within the school and beyond

[a] The educational systems of the following countries were studied: Belgium, Denmark, France, Germany, Greece, Ireland, Italy, Luxembourg, the Netherlands, Portugal, Spain, the United Kingdom, Austria, Finland, Sweden, Cyprus, the Czech Republic, Estonia, Hungary, Latvia, Lithuania, Malta, Poland, Slovakia, Slovenia and Romania

The audiences at these conferences not only had the opportunity to learn about the SEAs through presentations by researchers but also those by the end-users of these SEAs, who had participated in the research and reported on the impact the SEAs were having on their lives. Marta, a 10-year-old student at one of the successful schools studied by the project, explained how the *interactive groups* and the *dialogic literary gatherings* functioned at her school, where children now perform better academically and emotionally. Marta gave evidence of the gains created by those actions by sharing numerous examples involving her classmates. Among the stories she shared was the case of Aishan, a child who was in her class when they were 3 years old and had to leave for Senegal with his family 2 years later. He did not attend school during the time he spent in Senegal, and when he returned to Spain during the fourth grade, instead of being placed in a separate classroom with a curriculum with lower learning objectives, he was included in the regular classroom in *interactive groups*. Thanks to this policy he was not left behind and is gradually becoming able to keep up with the pace of his peers as they become friends.

Similarly, at the Final Conference Manuel, a family member from La Paz school, one of the case studies analyzed as a part of INCLUD-ED, explained the enormous improvement experienced in his school after the SEAs had been in place for 5 years. The school substantially reduced early school leaving, overcame absenteeism, improved students' academic outcomes as measured in official external evaluations, and eradicated conflicts, thereby fostering social cohesion in the community. Given these outcomes, the school became a model for the community of what could be performed in other areas of the neighborhood to overcome poverty. Thereby, a transformation of health, housing, social and political participation, etc. was initiated based on the successful actions. The transformations being achieved in this regard are enormous, changing the present and future of youths and adults in the barrio (Aubert 2011). Thus, Manuel concluded his speech to the European Parliament with the following moving sentence: *From here I want to say to all the parents and children of the world that if we had the misfortune of being poor and living in difficult areas, we can also change because we need it, society can see how we can get out of poverty.*

The successful actions that resulted in these improvements in the lives of Marta and Manuel are explained in the following chapters.

References

Aubert, A. (2011). Moving beyond social exclusion through dialogue. *International Studies in Sociology of Education, 21*(1), 63–75.

European Commission. (2011). Conclusions of the "Science Against Poverty" EU Conference. Retrieved November 29, 2013, from http://www.scienceagainstpoverty.es/Publico/Resultados/conclusiones/__Recursos/Draft-Conclusions_summary.pdf

Garfinkel, H. (1967). *Studies in ethnomethodology.* New Jersey: Prentice-Hall.

Gómez, A., Puigvert, L., & Flecha, R. (2011). Critical communicative methodology: Informing real social transformation through research. *Qualitative Inquiry, 17*(3), 235–245.

Habermas, J. (1984). *The theory of communicative action. Reason and the rationalization of society*, vol.1. Boston: Beacon Press.

Mead, G. H. (1934). *Mind, self and society*. Chicago: University of Chicago Press.

Schütz, A., & Luckmann, T. (1973). *The structures of the life-world*. London: Heinemann.

Touraine, A., Wieviorka, M., & Flecha, R. (2004). *Conocimiento e Identidad. Voces de grupos culturales en la investigación social*. Barcelona: El Roure.

Valls, R., & Padrós, M. (2011). Using dialogic research to overcome poverty: From principles to action. *European Journal of Education, 46*(2), 173–183.

Chapter 3
Forms of Classroom Arrangement: Streaming, Mixture, Inclusion

On the basis of approaches to grouping pupils and organizing human resources, INCLUD-ED identified three different forms of classroom arrangement. *Streaming* is defined by providing different curriculum standards to groups of pupils based on their ability and separating "different" students through ability grouping or placing them in special groups outside the classroom with additional teachers. *Streaming* is a response to *mixture*, the traditional arrangement where all students are grouped together, where the students are typically diverse in terms of levels of educational attainment, language proficiency, cultural background, and other factors. Both *streaming* and *mixture* lead to social exclusion. In contrast, *inclusion* involves heterogeneous groupings and does not separate pupils according to their ability. Indeed, the use of *inclusion* encourages the practice of peer help and has been proven to increase learning interaction, self-esteem, mutual respect, solidarity, acceptance of diversity and lead to high expectations. Existing human resources that would otherwise be devoted to *streaming* practices to separate students are instead used in inclusive classrooms to improve all pupils' outcomes.

This chapter is based on an intensive review of European educational systems, including educational reforms, theories and outcomes. This research conducted through INCLUD-ED made it possible to clarify three different forms of classroom arrangement, according to the ways in which pupils are grouped and human resources are organized: *mixture, streaming, and inclusion*. Distinguishing among these three forms is a necessary step in identifying which actions are truly Successful Educational Actions. Classroom grouping practices can vary substantially depending on variables such as students' age, the subjects taught, learning tasks, the level of support available in class, the extent to which interaction among students is promoted or the sizes of the groups (Baines et al. 2003). After reviewing systems and practices across Europe, the INCLUD-ED project identified *mixture*, *streaming* and *inclusion* as the three main types of classroom arrangement, which allowed us to distinguish Successful Educational Actions from unsuccessful ones.

© The Author(s) 2015
R. Flecha (Ed.), INCLUD-ED Consortium, *Successful Educational Actions for Inclusion and Social Cohesion in Europe*, SpringerBriefs in Education,
DOI 10.1007/978-3-319-11176-6_3

Streaming[1] is defined as providing different curriculum standards to different groups of pupils based on their ability, a practice that occurs within schools (European Commission 2006). At present, *streaming* is a common practice in Europe; it began as a response to traditional classrooms, in which a single teacher is responsible for a number of pupils who are typically diverse in terms of their levels of educational attainment, language proficiency, cultural background, and other characteristics. Under the traditional arrangement, which we term *mixture*, it would not be possible for the teacher to respond to the diversity observed in classrooms, and schools began to implement *streaming* practices, separating "different" students through ability grouping or placing them in special groups outside the classroom with additional teachers. Thus, these additional teachers teach groups of pupils that are homogenous with respect to ability. Both *streaming* and *mixture* produce school failure and therefore lead to social exclusion.

Researchers have provided extensive evidence that *streaming* does not contribute to school success. Various studies have demonstrated that *streaming* increases the differences in performance among pupils, and thus it does not improve their overall performance (Terwel 2005). High achievers may benefit from *streaming*, or it may have no effect on their attainment. However, in streamed classrooms, low achievers learn less because they spend less time on instructional activities, the material and content they are exposed to is less challenging, instruction is of lower quality and the pace of instruction slower (Braddock and Slavin 1992; Ireson et al. 2005; Terwel 2005).

Finally, *streaming* limits the opportunities for upward mobility between streams and reduces students' satisfaction with their stream placement (Hallinan 1996; Hallam and Ireson 2007). It is highly likely that children belonging to vulnerable groups will be assigned to low-achieving groups (Braddock and Slavin 1992; Hallinan 1996; Lucas and Berends 2002), and this contributes to students being segregated, categorized, stigmatized, and socially stratified (Hallam et al. 2004; Wiliam and Bartholomew 2004; Terwel 2005). The same is true for children with disabilities, whose attainment levels may decline even further (Dunn 1968).

> *Streaming* reduces pupils' learning opportunities and achievement by reducing the peer effect that higher-ability pupils have on their lower-ability classmates (Zimmer 2003). *Streaming* also reduces the expectations of those

---

[1] This practice has been analyzed for many years, and a range of terms have been used to refer to it, among those terms are streaming, curriculum differentiation, ability grouping, and in certain contexts, tracking and setting. In this publication, we emphasize actions which coincide with the European Commission's definition of streaming. In the UK the term "setting" is used to refer to a form of what in this publication is called "streaming". In other contexts, such as the United States, the term "tracking" is also used to refer to what is understood as "streaming" in Europe. For "tracking" we will take the definition of the European Commission (2006), which refers to separating students into different schools based on ability, often involving a division into academic/ general and vocational tracks.

in lower-ability groups and tends to erode their academic self-esteem and feelings of competence (Hallam et al. 2004).

Recent international surveys such as PISA, TIMSS and PIRLS contributed further results to this body of scientific evidence. However, these international surveys compare *streaming* with both *mixture* and *inclusion*, as if the latter two options were identical. For example, the PISA survey asks teachers whether they group students into different groups based on ability or if they do so within a single classroom. When teachers answer in the affirmative, the conclusion is that they are using *streaming*. Teachers who employ either *mixture* or *inclusion* actions would respond negatively to that question, and therefore *mixture* and *inclusion* are considered identical. Nonetheless, *mixture* and *inclusion* lead to very different educational situations and learning experiences, and therefore each of them produces very different results in terms of achievement. Thus, one of the main challenges in collecting data on *inclusion* involves clarifying whether heterogeneous grouping involves the reallocation of resources (*inclusion*) or not (*mixture*).

It is necessary to differentiate between *mixture* and *inclusion* based on the role and use of resources in schools and classrooms, as research has demonstrated that the availability of resources is important in determining student performance but it does not automatically improve educational attainment. What is relevant is not the amount of resources available but how these resources are organized and spent (Hanushek and Wößmann 2006). International quantitative data have shown that countries with similar levels of investment per student have different educational results. Conversely, countries with similar scores on international evaluations spend very different amounts on education (OECD 2007). Overall, resources (measured as investments in education) can only explain approximately 19 % of student performance (OECD 2007).

This indicates that when analyzing the relationship between student performance and types of student groupings, it is important to not only consider placement based on ability but also the way in which resources are used. In this regard, some *streaming* practices imply the use of additional resources (e.g., support teachers) to assist low-performing students, but those resources are allocated to ability groups or students in segregated classrooms. In contrast, certain inclusionary actions ensure that human resources are allocated to regular classrooms that had previously gone to segregated classrooms and low-achieving students. The use of resources in a *streaming* setting does not improve the achievement of all students, it increases the differences in achievement between high and low achievers; the reallocation of resources in inclusive learning environments raises the achievement of all students (Table 3.1).

The project's analysis of educational reforms in Europe led to the creation of a classification that includes *four different types of streaming* (Table 3.2). All types entail adapting the curriculum to students' prior knowledge or level of attainment and separating them based on ability. First, through the *organization of classroom*

Table 3.1 Characteristics of *mixture*, *streaming* and *inclusion* based on student grouping and resource allocations rationales

	Mixture	Streaming	Inclusion	
Basis	Equal opportunity	Difference	Equality of results/equality of differences	
Student grouping	Heterogeneous	Homogeneous	Heterogeneous	
Human resources	1 teacher	More than 1 teacher	More than 1 teacher	
All together or separated?	Together	Separate	Together	Separate
	(1) Mixed-ability classrooms	(1) Classroom activities are organized according to ability level	(1) Hetero-geneous ability classrooms with a reallocation of resources	(2) Inclusive split classes with mixed-ability students
		a. Different ability groups in different classrooms		
		b. All ability groups in the same classroom		
		(2) Remedial groups and support systems are separated from the regular classroom		

activities according to ability levels, groups of higher and lower performers are created within the classroom or in different classrooms. These groups are generally employed in compulsory core subjects (i.e., math, reading) and thus can have a greater effect on students' educational success, particularly for individuals in vulnerable groups. In the second type, *remedial groups and segregated support*, additional support is provided to pupils with particular needs, segregating them from the regular classroom during school hours. This type of support is often provided for pupils with disabilities, migrant pupils, pupils belonging to cultural minorities, and those who are generally not performing as well as their peers. Third, under an *exclusionary, individualized curriculum*, the curriculum is adapted to the level of a particular student or a group, lowering the standards to be achieved in one or several subjects. Fourth, in *exclusionary choice*, the school offers a choice of curricular subjects that leads to unequal future academic and social opportunities.

As in *mixture*, *inclusion* involves heterogeneous groupings and does not separate pupils according to their ability or school performance. However, it differs from *mixture* in that it responds to the diversity found in the student body through particular inclusive actions that aim to support low achievers' learning and primarily draws on existing human resources that a *streaming* system would use to separate students. The academic literature highlights the positive effects of working in heterogeneous groups. Several researchers have found that heterogeneous grouping contributes to improving pupils' outcomes and to reducing the differences

Table 3.2 Types of *streaming*

Types of streaming	Description
1. Organization of classroom activities according to ability levels	Teaching should be adapted to students' different needs and paces
	Higher- and lower-performing students are grouped separately in the same classroom or in different ones
	Ability groups are typically implemented to teach core subjects. They are most often used in secondary education and usually precede further tracking
	This grouping can have a negative impact on students' educational success and social inclusion
	They are often based on individual teachers' or schools' decisions
	Members of vulnerable groups are often assigned to low-achieving educational groups
2. Remedial groups and support services segregated from the regular classroom	Created for children with particular learning needs or for those at risk of social exclusion
	Students are segregated from the regular classroom during school hours to receive additional support
	This action is most often used for students in special education, along with immigrant students, members of cultural minority groups, and those who have not mastered the language of instruction
	Ultimately results in the labeling of students and reducing the level of instruction
3. Exclusionary individualized curriculum	The official curriculum is adapted to the level of competence of a particular student (or group of students), reducing the level of rigor
	This approach is often used for specific groups of students: those assigned to special education, immigrants, and language learners
4. Exclusionary choice	Selecting a subject or a group of subjects leads to unequal future academic and social opportunities
	When this occurs, the choice of subjects or "streams" is often strongly associated with the family's social and economic status and the teacher's expectations

between attainment levels in diverse classrooms (Braddock and Slavin 1992; Boaler 2006). They also indicate that low achievers benefit from the pace of instruction used for high-achieving pupils, demonstrating positive results in classroom arrangements that feature cooperative learning (Cesar and Santos 2006; Schroeder et al. 2007). In addition, *inclusion* actions promote self-esteem, mutual respect, solidarity, and the acceptance of diversity (in terms of disability, culture, gender, and attainment level), as well as collaboration and altruism (Slavin 1991; Johnson et al. 1994; Stevens and Slavin 1995; Elboj et al. 2002).

> *Inclusion* practices include peer help through increased interaction, support from volunteers and family members in the classroom, accounting for cultural intelligences and promoting dialogic learning (Elboj et al. 2002). *Inclusion* also includes additional support in the classroom and *extending learning time* for low achievers, along with high expectations and assigning roles, competences, and responsibilities (Braddock and Slavin 1992; Boaler 2006; Lotan 2006).

Another important aspect of inclusive classrooms is that they maintain the same standards for all pupils, and this can be ensured through the promotion of interactive and group work (Stevens and Slavin 1995; Stainback and Stainback 1996; Porter 1997; Blatchford et al. 2003; Meijer et al. 2003; Koutrouba et al. 2006). All of these inclusive strategies are implemented in heterogeneous groupings.

In particular, when heterogeneous classrooms are organized appropriately and the necessary resources are provided, pupils with disabilities perform better academically and have a better self-concept compared to those in segregated classrooms (Luster and Durret 2003; Fitch 2003; Myklebust 2006). Moreover, pupils with disabilities have greater opportunities to interact with more capable peers in heterogeneous groups, to receive greater support, and to develop better social skills and relationships; thus, they are better prepared to be more independent in the future (Hess et al. 2006). Furthermore, the inclusion of pupils with disabilities has positive effects on their peers' performance and provides new learning opportunities (McGregor and Vogelsberg 1998; Fisher et al. 2002). INCLUD-ED has identified *different types of inclusion* (Table 3.3).

The definition of inclusive actions and their differences from *mixture* and *streaming* actions was a necessary step for identifying Successful Educational Actions (SEAs), which is the major contribution of the INCLUD-ED project. These actions were identified through the research conducted for projects 1, 2 and 6. In those projects, INCLUD-ED researchers analyzed educational systems, theories, and outcomes and contrasted them with an analysis of successful schools across Europe, some of which involve empowering forms of family and community participation.

SEAs lead to both efficiency and equity; that is, they allow schools to achieve solid educational results for all students, especially those who are at greater risk of social exclusion. The SEAs were identified in schools located in low socio-economic status contexts, which serve students with migrant and/or minority backgrounds (Mircea and Sordé 2011) and realize high levels of student educational attainment relative to schools with similar socio-cultural and socio-economic characteristics. According to the analysis of these successful schools, the implementation of SEAs explains the success that these schools achieve. In one of the selected schools, for example, in the

Table 3.3 Types of *inclusion*

Types of inclusion	Description
1. Heterogeneous ability classrooms with a reallocation of human resources	Consists of providing greater support through reallocated resources in regular classrooms containing diverse students. Generally, the teaching staff provides this support, although family and community members can also assist in the classroom
	In most cases, the reallocated support is provided for specific groups of students, such as those who are considered to require special education, immigrant students, pupils who are members of minority groups, and those with language-related difficulties. This support enables them to remain in the regular classroom
2. Inclusive split classes	Different teachers are responsible for different heterogeneous groups of students. An inclusive split classroom would involve, for instance, two heterogeneous groups of students containing 12 students and one teacher each
	This is often employed for specific subjects (e.g., languages and mathematics), allows the classroom to be organized differently, and reduces the student-teacher ratio
3. Extended learning time	The provision of additional learning time or academic activities is more common for students who live in socially disadvantaged areas or have a minority background
	This can be implemented, for example, through a longer school day, students and families receiving assistance through family support or private lessons at school or in the home, or offering educational activities during holiday periods and after regular school hours throughout the school year
4. Inclusive, individualized curriculum	The inclusive, individualized curriculum is not intended to reduce the knowledge that a student has to acquire. Instead, the teaching methods are adapted to facilitate the student's learning and the activities included are addressed to move the student toward higher levels of achievement
5. Inclusive choice	It is not based on students' abilities but on their preferences, and it does not lead to a dead end
	It does not reduce students' subsequent educational and social opportunities; instead, equal opportunities are guaranteed after making this choice

period between 2001 and 2007, the percentage of students who achieved basic competence in reading comprehension rose from 17 to 85 %; this occurred while the number of students of migrant origin increased from 12 to 46 % (Fig. 3.1). These

Fig. 3.1 The improvement in reading skills achievement in one of the successful schools studied

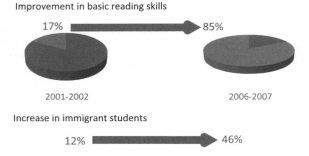

results dispel long-standing assumptions associating low academic achievement with the migrant composition of a school's student body.

> INCLUD-ED demonstrates that it is not the characteristics of the students, their families or the neighborhood that explain the results achieved by those pupils; but the actions being implemented in the schools they attend. When the schools implement SEAs, educational performance improves.

INCLUD-ED identified two primary groups of Successful Educational Actions. The first is based on specific approaches to grouping pupils and allocating human resources, according to *inclusive actions*. The second group of SEAs is *successful types of family and community participation* in schools, which promote school success. Both types of SEAs are explained in the following chapters.

References

Baines, E., Blatchford, P., & Kutnick, P. (2003). Changes in grouping practices over primary and secondary school. *International Journal of Educational Research, 39*, 9–34.

Blatchford, P., Kutnick, P., Baines, E., & Galton, M. (2003). Toward a social pedagogy of classroom group work. *International Journal of Educational Research, 39*, 153–172.

Braddock, J. H., & Slavin, R. E. (1992). *Why ability grouping must end: Achieving excellence and equity in American education*. Baltimore, MD: Center for Research on Effective Schooling for Disadvantaged Pupils.

Boaler, J. (2006). How a detracked mathematics approach promoted respect, responsibility and high achievement. *Theory Into Practice, 45*(1), 40–46.

Cesar, M., & Santos, N. (2006). From exclusion to inclusion: Collaborative work contributions to more inclusive learning settings. *European Journal of Psychology of Education, 21*(3), 333–346.

Dunn, L. M. (1968). Special education for the mildly retarded. Is much of it justifiable? *Exceptional Children, 35*(1), 5–22.

Elboj, C., Puigdellívol, I., Soler, M., & Valls, R. (2002). *Comunidades de aprendizaje. Transformar la educación*. Barcelona: Graó.

European Commission. (2006). Commission staff working document. Accompanying document to the *Communication from the Commission to the Council and to the European Parliament. Efficiency and equity in European education and training systems.* SEC(2006) 1096, Brussels, September 2006.

Fisher, D., Roach, V., & Frey, N. (2002). Examining the general programmatic benefits of inclusive schools. *International Journal of Inclusive Education, 6*(1), 63–78.

Fitch, F. (2003). Inclusion, exclusion, and ideology: Special education pupils' changing sense of self. *The Urban Review, 35*(3), 233–252.

Hallam, S., Ireson, J., & Davies, J. (2004). Primary pupils' experiences of different types of grouping in school. *British Educational Research Journal, 30*(4), 515–533.

Hallam, S., & Ireson, J. (2007). Secondary school pupils' satisfaction with their ability grouping placements. *British Educational Research Journal, 33*(1), 27–45.

Hallinan, M. T. (1996). Track mobility in secondary school. *Social Forces, 74*(3), 983–1002.

Hanushek A.E., & Wößmann, L. (2006). Does educational tracking affect performance and inequality? Differences-in-differences evidence across countries. *Economic Journal, Royal Economic Society, 116* (510), C63–C76, 03.

Hess, R. S., Molina, A. M., & Kozleski, E. B. (2006). Until somebody hears me: parent voice and advocacy in special educational decision making. *British Journal of Special Education, 33*(3), 148–157.

Ireson, J., Hallam, S., & Hurley, C. (2005). What are the effects of ability grouping on GCSE attainment? *British Educational Research Journal, 31*(4), 443–458.

Johnson, D. W., Johnson, R. T., & Holubec, E. J. (1994). *Cooperative learning in the classroom.* Alexandria, VA: Association for Supervision and Curriculum.

Koutrouba, K., Vamvakari, M., & Steliou, M. (2006). Factors correlated with teachers' attitudes towards the inclusion of pupils with special educational needs in Cyprus. *European Journal of Special Needs Education, 21*(4), 381–394.

Lotan, R. A. (2006). Teaching teachers to build equitable classrooms. *Theory Into Practice, 45*(1), 32–39.

Lucas, S., & Berends, M. (2002). Sociodemographic diversity, correlated achievement, and de facto tracking. *Sociology of Education, 75*(4), 328–348.

Luster, J.N., & Durret, J. (2003). Does educational placement matter in the performance of pupils with disabilities? *Paper presented at the Annual Meeting of the Mid-South Educational Research Association.*

McGregor, G., & Vogelsberg, R. T. (1998). *Inclusive schooling practices: pedagogical and research foundations. A synthesis of the literature that informs best practices about inclusive schooling.* Pittsburg, PA: Allegheny University of Health Sciences.

Meijer, C., Soriano, V., & Watkins, A. (Eds.). (2003). *Special Needs Education in Europe.* Denmark: Thematic Publication, European Agency for Development in Special Needs Education.

Mircea, T., & Sordé, T. (2011). How to turn difficulties into opportunities: drawing from diversity to promote social cohesion. *International Studies in Sociology of Education, 21*(1), 49–62.

Myklebust, J. O. (2006). Class placement and competence attainment among pupils with special educational needs. *British Journal of Special Education, 33*(2), 76–81.

OECD, Organization for Economic Co-operation and Development. (2007). *PISA 2006 science competencies for tomorrow's world: Results from PISA 2006,* No. 1, OECD. Retrieved January 20, 2011 from http://www.pisa.oecd.org/dataoecd/30/17/39703267.pdf.

Porter, G. L. (1997). Critical elements for inclusive schools. In S. J. Pijl, C. J. W. Meijer, & S. Hegerty (Eds.), *Inclusive Education, a Global Agenda* (pp. 68–81). London: Routledge Publishing.

Schroeder, C., Scott, T. P., Tolson, H., Huang, T., & Lee, Y. (2007). A meta-analysis of national research: Effects of teaching strategies on student achievement in science in the United States. *Journal of Research in Science Teaching, 44*(10), 1436–1460.

Slavin, R. (1991). Synthesis of research of cooperative learning. *Educational Leadership, 48*(5), 71–82.

Stainback, S., & Stainback, W. (Eds.). (1996). *Curriculum Considerations In Inclusive Classrooms: Facilitating Learning for All Pupils.* Baltimore: Paul H. Brookes Pub.

Stevens, R., & Slavin, R. (1995). The cooperative elementary school: Effects on pupils' achievement, attitudes, and social relations. *American Educational Research Journal, 32*(2), 321–351.

Terwel, J. (2005). Curriculum differentiation: Multiple perspectives and developments in education. *Journal of Curriculum Studies, 37*(6), 653–670.

Wiliam, D., & Bartholomew, H. (2004). It's not which school but which set you're in that matters: The influence of ability grouping practices on student progress in mathematics. *British Educational Research Journal, 30*(2), 279–293.

Zimmer, R. (2003). New twist in the educational tracking debate. *Economics of Education Review, 22*(3), 307–315.

Chapter 4
Successful Educational Actions In/Outside the Classroom

The Successful Educational Actions (SEAs) have demonstrated their ability to achieve excellent results with respect to academic success and increased social cohesion in different schools with diverse student bodies and families. Of these actions, we highlight *interactive groups* (heterogeneous groups of pupils with one adult volunteer per group who promotes peer interaction), *dialogic reading* (a new understanding of the reading event that involves reading with more individuals, in more spaces and times) and *extended learning time* (after school programs such as homework clubs or tutored libraries). In addition to describing these actions and the reorganization of human resources they entail, this chapter will provide concrete data on pupils' results following the implementation of the aforementioned SEAs.

Two features of SEAs help to achieve the objective of school success for all pupils: (1) the creation of heterogeneous groups that include pupils with different mastery levels and (2) the reorganization of human resources to cater to the needs of all pupils within a single classroom.

Based on these two features, SEAs make it possible to achieve maximum results with existing resources. INCLUD-ED provides evidence that educating all students need not involve increasing economic resources. We studied 20 schools in 6 different countries covering pre-primary, primary and secondary education, special education programs in regular schools and vocational training programs. These schools served a high proportion of students with low socioeconomic status and migrant and minority backgrounds, and made a demonstrated contribution to the students' school success and achieved better results than other, similarly situated schools. The schools studied did not experience improved results because they received additional resources, but because they organized available resources (both those in the schools and the community) more effectively and obtained the greatest possible value from them. The same resources can be used to separate students according to their learning level or to include everyone in regular classrooms. Reallocating existing resources previously dedicated to separating students to implement inclusive actions leads to success for all. Inclusive groupings can also include volunteers from the community, an approach that maximizes both the available resources and the students' learning possibilities.

© The Author(s) 2015   31
R. Flecha (Ed.), INCLUD-ED Consortium, *Successful Educational Actions for Inclusion and Social Cohesion in Europe*, SpringerBriefs in Education,
DOI 10.1007/978-3-319-11176-6_4

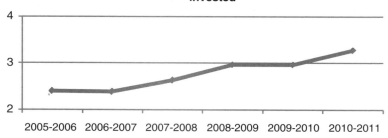

Fig. 4.1 Number of students educated per each 1,000 € invested per month in the period between 2005–2006 and 2010–2011

As an illustration, in one of the school cases studied, in a 5-year period (2005–2006 to 2010–2011), as SEAs were implemented, the number of enrolled students increased to a much greater extent than the number of teachers. As a consequence, the number of students allocated to each teacher increased from an average of 5.88–8.05. During the same period, student achievement levels improved dramatically; only one year after the school began to implement SEAs, student test scores doubled in six competencies. The school maintained this progress. These data demonstrate that implementing SEAs allowed existing resources to be used more efficiently. This is reflected in the number of students taught at the school for each 1,000 € of monthly expenditures, which increased from 2.39 to 3.28 (Fig. 4.1). While the school spent less per pupil, the results improved due to the implementation of the SEAs.

The inclusive actions identified here were those implemented the most completely and carefully in the successful schools the project studied.

4.1   Interactive Groups

Interactive groups have been found to be a very successful form of heterogeneous-ability classrooms with human resources appropriately reallocated. This type of *inclusion* entails that diverse pupils are grouped together in the regular classroom, creating heterogeneous groups with respect to pupils' ability, ethnicity, gender, and disabilities. Then, the school considers its existing human resources (for instance, support teachers, especial education teachers, language experts, mediators, family members, volunteers, etc.) and reorganizes them to provide the support the pupils require within the classroom. Rather than using these human resources to separate children and provide them with an adapted curriculum, these professionals and volunteers are involved in the regular classroom and provide support to pupils there. The result is that more adults are present in the classroom, meaning greater cognitive resources for all children to learn more effectively.

The reorganization of human resources inside the classroom helps lower achievers to increase the pace of their learning, which is especially important for disadvantaged children. Moreover, it also has a positive impact on the class as a whole. By providing in-classroom support, inclusive actions allow teachers to teach the same curriculum to all pupils and facilitate individualized support.

> The reorganization of human resources occurs in different ways in the schools we analyzed: individual support (more adults) to children with special needs, inclusive split classes, or *interactive groups*. Among the different *inclusion* actions we studied, we found that organizing the class into *interactive groups* led to the most improvement (Elboj and Niemelä 2010; Oliver and Gatt 2010).

In the case of *interactive groups* (Fig. 4.2), the heterogeneous classroom is organized into small and heterogeneous groups of pupils (e.g., four groups of five pupils) and includes several adults, one per group. Each group works on an activity that involves learning core subjects for approximately 20 min. Then, the groups rotate and work on a different activity with a different adult. These adults are other teachers, family members, volunteers from the community, and other volunteers; they are responsible for fostering interactions among the children to solve the assigned tasks, and they also expose the students to a wider and richer range of learning interactions. The classroom teacher manages overall classroom activity and provides additional support when necessary.

In interactive groups, children learn in interaction with their peers, who have various ability levels; some of the students are stronger academically. The groups provide additional opportunities for mutual help among children with different learning levels and paces, as well as with a wide range of diverse adults. In *interactive groups*, academically strong pupils become a resource to help the others.

Fig. 4.2 *Interactive groups*, the classroom is organized into small and heterogeneous groups of pupils and includes adults, one per group

Moreover, this approach guarantees that the highest performers are not forced to wait while the others catch up, but instead continue advancing in their learning because they reinforce their metacognitive abilities when they explain how to successfully solve the task to others. Making individual thinking public raises the more advanced students' awareness of their knowledge; this causes them to identify misunderstandings and gaps in their thinking and deepen their understandings of abstract concepts and procedures. Thereby, the increased communicative and supportive interactions accelerate learning for all pupils and promote solidarity among classmates.

In the schools studied that employ *interactive groups*, teachers highlighted the benefits provided by this dialogic organization of learning. They highlighted how interactions among classmates increased the knowledge of all students participating in an activity. Both the student who helps or provides explanations to a classmate and the student receiving the explanation benefit from this process of intersubjective meaning-making. The following quote from a teacher exemplifies this:

> Those who help definitely learn as well. Let's see, if a boy has to explain a problem to his classmate and he knows how to do it (…) he does it well, no? However, when he explains it he has to go through a small reflection process in his head, to lower his level of understanding, let's say, and then communicate it verbally to his classmates so that they can understand it. Therefore, this is a reasoning process that he goes through and that really helps him to learn more and become aware of what he knows, you see? Because by verbalizing knowledge, one learns a lot too. It is when you really… when you have to describe something that you think you know that you really become aware of what you know about that, you see? And that well… I think that that is wonderful for children. (Teacher)

Families confirm the academic improvements observed in their children since they began participating in *interactive groups*. As many of these families are also volunteers in the school, they have been able to observe these improvements not only in their own children but also in other students. This is the case for Elena, the mother of a child in one of the schools, who has participated as a volunteer in classroom activities for many years. Based on her experience, she can describe the way in which *interactive groups* increase the level of attention devoted to each child in the teaching-learning process. This mother stated that there is an increase in individualized attention in the learning process, thanks to the support that every child receives from both peers and adults. Both are key elements in improving academic performance:

> It is about the fact that these 5 or 6 children at the table are looking at you, they look at you intently and they are attentive to you, they don't get distracted by the others at the other table; it is like being at home with your child at your table and being attentive to your child, it is very similar [although] with four more children, I don't know, it seems like you are more on top of them and it seems like they get it more. (Family member)

As the teachers explained, apart from having a strong positive impact on academic results, the *interactive groups* also have repercussions for the students' acquisition and consolidation of certain values. In *interactive groups*, it has been demonstrated that the pursuit of each individual's academic success does not lead to greater competitiveness among students, but on the contrary, it generates greater solidarity.

The volunteers play a crucial role in this regard. The dynamic created by the collaboration among volunteers constantly promotes interaction among the various classmates in the group, as well as fostering the dynamics of mutual aid though dialogue. The group members rapidly come to understand that individual success is attained when everyone in the group solves the task successfully. Consequently, collaborating in *interactive groups* promotes the development of solidarity in social relations. Therefore, our analysis of *interactive groups* in successful schools demonstrated that it is not necessary to choose between learning core academic subjects and learning values, such as solidarity; both can be learnt together in the same framework. Moreover, the experience that teachers shared during our fieldwork revealed that solidarity learnt through *interactive groups* was subsequently transferred to other learning contexts, as the following teacher explains:

> When they are working, you try to ensure that the one who is helping… the idea of *interactive groups* is not only used when *interactive groups* are being employed, but the idea that when someone finishes an exercise, well, you help the other one, or try to help. The children offer themselves when they are finished; they are already in the habit of thinking: "I've already finished so I can help that one over there". Well, that is palpable, helping each other and so on. (Teacher)

Interactive groups also increase the academic expectations of both teachers and pupils. On the one hand, this gain is due to the improvement in all pupils' learning outcomes, which in turn improves students' self concepts as learners (Gatt et al. 2010). They have greater trust in their potential to continue studying beyond school and have better jobs. On the other hand, it is important that the roles played by all of the educational agents who participate in the children's learning process ensure that every pupil gains confidence in his or her potential. Every new adult in the classroom means new opportunities to create new interactions and new academic concepts and expectations. In the following quote, a teacher reflected on the new expectations created by the participation of university volunteers:

> Before, [when asked] "What do you want to do?" the children said "To be a builder, my father is a builder". "I want to be a truck-driver because my father is a truck-driver". But now, for example, I have a child whose name is Antonio who says that he wants to be a teacher. Why? Because he can see volunteers who come in who are university people, they are studying and we also explain to them "look… here's Lidia [a volunteer] who is in the university and she would like to be a teacher one day and teach other teachers too so that they can then teach children". Or the Arabic teacher "well look he is a teacher", he is Moroccan, but you see for Moroccan children, well, he is also a role model because Moroccan children, when you ask them, well, they don't tell you what their parents do, you see? They want to… but normally in these families they don't have degrees, no? Therefore, this is very interesting. (Teacher)

This example demonstrates that *interactive groups* provide children with different role models. All types of adults provide assistance in the *interactive groups*: autochthonous and foreign families, university students, teachers from their schools or from other schools, nuns, Arab women, etc. The greater the diversity of the classroom volunteers, the more possible it is to overcome stereotypes, including those related to culture and gender. Laura, the head teacher at one school, supported this understanding of the impact of involving volunteers with different profiles in overcoming cultural and gender-related stereotypes:

> We had Fatima, a Moroccan female university student, collaborating for a while; she had studied in the US, and of course when she was coming here she was a high-level role model, above all for the young Moroccan girls, but the other girls and boys also had a Moroccan academic role model, who was Moroccan in origin, and then of course that played a role and meant we were dealing with a great deal of issues without explicitly dealing with them because they experienced it, and the idea was introduced that at least that person could serve as an example. If [some students] said bad things about Moroccan people and said that they are all beggars, [other students] could say, well Fatima is studying and she is at the university. (Teacher)

The findings confirmed that when schools engage in SEAs such as *interactive groups* and devote additional human resources within the classroom structure of *interactive groups*, there is a positive impact on the achievement of all students and especially on disadvantaged groups. Often, these improvements result from taking advantage of resources coming from disadvantaged communities, such as migrants and certain cultural groups, who have much to contribute intellectually and culturally to schools. The interactions migrant students engage in when collaborating with their non-immigrant peers allow them to accelerate their learning, and this allows them to improve substantially. Closing the achievement gap between different groups of students is beneficial for the entire school and creates a sense of belonging and solidarity among the students, which also contributes to overcoming cultural segregation.

> The subject of the *interactive groups* we do here, (…) it is one of the activities (…) which works best for us. (…) we now have two girls who arrived just now at Easter from Latin America, and today I gave them a reading comprehension test and they are within normal levels. (…) I am happy with the *interactive groups* or with those types of activities that really involve them helping each other. Peer learning… I am very happy [with that] and perhaps part of the proof is [provided by] these children. (Teacher)

Furthermore, the inclusion of students with special needs in the classroom is a positive learning experience for all students. This also takes place in *interactive groups*. The use of additional resources in *interactive groups* in the classroom improves the integration of students with special educational needs. Students with disabilities participate in the same learning activities thanks to the support received by other students, who include more capable peers, and both the students with special needs and the other students benefitted from the assistance provided by the additional human resources, i.e., volunteers and other teachers, including the special education teacher. Therefore, specific support (such as the special education teacher) becomes less necessary, and students with special educational needs participate in the activity with no distinction between them and the rest of the class. As one teacher noted, it is difficult for some students with greater difficulties or a specific problem to accept additional support when it is specifically addressed to them. However, when this support is provided to everyone through *interactive groups*, they are more likely to accept it. This is the opposite of receiving additional support in a segregated classroom.

So, because in *interactive groups*, there is an adult at each table, it means that it is not strange for you have one [adult there] and they help you more. You are the same as the others. While [on the other hand] inside the [regular] classroom, no matter how normal it is [for this to happen], that person helps you to read [individually], and not the others. (Teacher)

Students with special educational needs become part of the regular class dynamics and have the opportunity to interact with their peers. They also enjoy more challenging opportunities and can access more academic material without creating a disadvantage for their peers, thereby avoiding negative labeling. This is possible because higher-ability students, or adults, can help them, and this solidarity-based learning process benefits both types of students.

4.2   Extending Learning Time

Extended learning time is an inclusive measure consisting of offering additional learning activities and support classes outside of regular school hours (i.e., at midday, after school, etc.). This option provides greater support for pupils who have difficulties or receive less support at home, without segregating them outside the regular classroom during school hours, which causes them to miss regular classroom activities and frequently the official curriculum. Through the case studies of successful schools throughout Europe, we identified several ways to implement this action and achieve positive outcomes. In some cases, teachers/educators support the pupils though *review classes, consultation hours,* or *extended-day groups.* In certain instances, this support is provided on the weekends and/or before high-stakes exams. In other cases, teachers provide language support by teaching the language of instruction to immigrant pupils. Similarly, learning support classes for pupils with disabilities are designed to accelerate their learning while they participate fully in regular classes.

Afterschool programs focused on learning core subjects have different names in different countries, such as *homework clubs* or *tutored libraries,* but they have the same objectives. Often, educators organize these learning spaces in collaboration with volunteers and community members, providing the opportunity to increase the number of pupils and the diversity of their interactions, which leads to increased learning (Tellado and Sava 2010). This is especially important in efforts to include children from vulnerable groups and those who cannot receive assistance with their homework at home, as activities that extend learning time and include additional adult support provide those children with further opportunities to pursue academic progress and reach the same level of attainment as their peers.

The activities conducted in these clubs are intended to reinforce the academic content taught in the classroom. Such activities were found to be especially important for pupils from disadvantaged backgrounds and those with disabilities. In Finland, the *homework club* is held from Mondays to Thursdays, after the school day and generally in the school building. It is voluntary and open to all pupils from every grade. It serves as an opportunity to reinforce learning because it offers additional support without separating pupils. As all children are welcome to the club, those with difficulties benefit from engaging in homework and support activities with peers and education assistants.

In Malta, the *after-school writing club* is organized based on collaboration between parents and pupils. The parent-student writing session was established in response to parents' requests. In this club, parents and children stay at school together after instructional hours with a professional educator; adults and children are jointly involved in writing activities designed to help parents understand what the writing process involves. As a result, students' reading and writing skills have improved.

In Spain, *tutored libraries* (Fig. 4.3) are organized after school hours. They provide learning support for pupils in reading, writing, math and languages assisting them with their homework. This type of support relies on the participation of volunteers, alumni, family members and other community members (occasionally from local associations). In the tutored libraries, the family members' participation makes it possible to extend the pupils' learning time.

The tutored library, if held outside school hours, ensures that students with low learning levels relative to their classmates have the opportunity to work more and with additional assistance and thereby reach the same level as their peers. One teacher explained it in this way:

> Of course it's good! When they leave the school building, imagine what it is like for those who do not stay behind in the tutored library. They go home and they have to do their homework, and well, perhaps they don't know how to do that homework and they have no one at home to help them with that homework. On the other hand, the ones who stayed got help because there were five of us in the library, and when they leave there they can then do something else because they've done their homework. It's very good. (Teacher)

In addition to the teachers, relatives also note the improvements achieved by their children as a result of participating in the tutored library. This is the case of

Fig. 4.3 *Tutored libraries* are organized after school hours. They provide learning support for pupils in reading, writing, math and languages

Patricia, a Colombian mother, who participates in this activity with other members of the community. She has observed a significant improvement in her child since he has begun receiving additional support in the tutored library. Patricia has become aware of the important role that the volunteers play in this activity:

> Apart from this, he has reinforcement in the tutored library, and Simón has advanced a lot, he has advanced a lot, but of course it's because he has instructors there, he has volunteers there because they are very much there for him, and for that reason I think that it helps a lot. (Family member)

The participation of volunteers in the tutored libraries diversifies students' learning interactions, as the adults volunteering in the library are not teachers or education professionals. Therefore, they help students and provide explanations and responses in a different way than teachers do in class (Valls and Kyriakides 2013). These explanations complement and enrich the students' learning process and, moreover, help them understand that learning does not only occur in class, during the school day and with teachers but can also occur after school hours and with many different adults and in different contexts. As a consequence, this practice has also transformed the relationship children have with learning, bringing learning interactions to other settings, such as the home.

4.3 Dialogic Reading

The "Matthew effect" is based on the notion that the more one has, the easier it is to have more. It has become a widely recognized effect in many areas. Merton (1968, 1973) introduced it in the field of sociology by demonstrating how scientists who are already recognized by the scientific community will typically receive more attention, even if their work is very similar to that of a less recognized scientist. Stanovich (1986) applied the concept to reading practices. For example, in the area of vocabulary, students with well-developed vocabulary skills are more likely to acquire new words than students with less rich vocabularies (Blachowicz and Obrochta 2005). Moreover, skilled readers will increasingly engage in reading activities, while poor readers' reading activities will become increasingly infrequent, thus increasing the gap between skilled and non-skilled readers. Importantly, instructional practices applied to learners who are struggling with reading often tend to decelerate the reading growth of these students instead of accelerating it (Blachowicz and Obrochta 2005). This is an exclusionary practice with far-reaching negative consequences, as other learning areas require reading skills to "read to learn". Therefore, children left behind in reading will also have difficulties in these other curricular areas.

The INCLUD-ED project identified *dialogic reading* as a SEA capable of overcoming the "Mathew Effect" in reading. *Dialogic reading* is an action that occurs in numerous, diverse contexts at more times (during schools hours and after school hours), in more spaces (from the classroom to the home and the street) and with more individuals (peers, friends, family members, teachers, neighbors, volunteers and other community members). Children from all social backgrounds improve their communicative abilities and reading levels. The acceleration of learning promoted by *dialogic reading* substantially depends on interactions. In *dialogic reading* activities, the diversity of learning interactions increases, both between children and between children and adults. *Dialogic reading* encourages discussions between peers and adults regarding what they have read, what they understood and what they did not, and different interpretations of the text are shared, all of which promote critical reflection (Wells 1989; Soler 2001, 2003–2005, 2004; Wells and Arauz 2006).

One way in which *dialogic reading* practices are implemented is by *extending learning time*. Some of the schools studied used tutored library sessions to increase reading activities after school hours and with diverse individuals: other students, teachers, relatives or other members of the community. Reading activities in this context have led to clear improvements in children's learning. For instance, a mother whose child participated in the tutored library observed a significant improvement in his reading and that the academic interactions initiated in that setting were subsequently transferred to the home context: the boy asked his mother to read him stories, as they do in school, and the mother and child now share learning activities in their living room, where they had never had any academic dialogue before:

> He loves it. He loves it. And when we get home he says, "mum, read me another of those stories that you read in school, go on", and we work at home in the same way. (Mother)

Another *dialogic reading* practice that includes parental participation is the *Parent Readers* program. In this program, the family members of children in their first years of school accompany their children in the mornings so that they can read with their children in the school. In that way, reading is individualized, thereby producing improved performance with respect to the children's reading abilities and motivation to learn. Family participation in helping their children learn to read and write ensures that the children read every day for a short time in classrooms, thus improving their reading level. Tania, head of studies in one school implementing this practice, explained the success achieved and noted that the children had improved their reading and were more motivated to learn to read because their families had been coming into the classrooms to help them. Specifically, the head of studies observed the greatest improvements among children whose parents participated in this program. Children who could not read before this practice was initiated began to read due to family participation in the classroom. This improvement in reading ensured that the students' attitudes regarding their after-school reading habits improved, and their motivation to go to school increased:

> The children are much more encouraged to learn. They take books home to read because they are already reading with their father or mother; also [there is the idea of] "I know how to read now" because before they did not know how to because they [just] learned this year. So of course, there have been [improvements] because they are more motivated, they want to come along. (Head of studies)

The students' academic results confirm the effectiveness of *dialogic reading*. School success in this school is reflected in the students' academic results from the 2006–2007 school year, when the SEAs were implemented. In 2006–2007, all competency averages were under 2 (over 5). After only one year, all of these indicators increased substantially. Students doubled their grades in nearly all of them. In terms of reading, the student average increased from 1.4 (over 5) in 2006–2007 to 3 just one year later. Speaking increased from 1.8 to 3.8 in the same period; writing rose from 0.5 to 2.8, and the use of language improved from 0.7 to 1.9.

Another *dialogic reading* practice observed in successful schools is *Reading Buddies*. It consists of pairing students from Grade 5 or 6 with students in pre-primary or the first grades of primary education. The older child helps the younger one with reading practices characterized by close interaction, and this reinforces learning for both the older and younger children. Different times and spaces are used to ensure that buddies read together. For instance, one school used the break time to allow Grade 6 students to go to the library to mentor the young children and help them improve their reading. Another school used a library hour for this purpose. The books in the library were organized based on their difficulty level to facilitate the students' choice of books.

> Another practice which (…) works very well is reading buddies. (…) what we do is to pair a kid from fifth year with a kid from P5 (…) and on Friday, when the older ones have their library hour, they get a storybook for [the younger student] (…) they describe it; we dedicate some time to that, and some of them stay in their classrooms, some of us come here to the library (…) It's not about the older ones teaching the younger ones to read, but they do help them to… [learn] through this reading process, and so they explain the story to them, and they [the older ones] read it, they talk about it. (Teacher)

Teachers gave very positive feedback on this practice. The younger children relied on the additional assistance to learn to read and were highly motivated by working with older children, who also became role models, and the Grade 6 students were excited about their responsibility, while they were simultaneously able to reinforce their literacy skills and develop values such as solidarity.

Finally, *dialogic reading* is operationalized through *dialogic literary gatherings* (Fig. 4.4), which involve reading classic works of world literature and sharing interpretations with the group. This activity is also conducted with families, as discussed in the next chapter, as a type of family and community education. However it is also conducted with children as an after-school activity or a part of the regular curriculum (Pulido and Zepa 2010; Serrano et al. 2010). Before the gathering, the children prepare for the reading at home. They take the book home and read it alone or with others. Then, they select a paragraph or an idea they particularly enjoyed or would like to share for some reason, and in this gathering, they explain the ideas they chose, why they chose them, and discuss the topics the others shared.

Marta, a 10-year-old pupil who participated in the INCLUD-ED Final Conference at the European Parliament, explained how *dialogic literary gatherings* help her and her classmates to learn to read better. This improvement is related to the effort they devoted to improving their reading, the motivation generated by classical literature and their ability to share their interpretations with other relevant

Fig. 4.4 Dialogic reading is
operationalized through
dialogic *literary gatherings*

individuals. The interactions, both with peers in the classroom and with others at home, related to the reading event clearly contributed to this increased motivation and making reading a more meaningful activity. While such gatherings are beneficial for all students, those with migrant backgrounds and whose mother tongue differs from the language of instruction particularly benefit from them.

> We like literary gatherings because we learn more. We learn more vocabulary and expressions and we learn to read. One example is two boys from my class, one is called Ayoub and the other Kavi, and thanks to the literary gatherings, they learned to read. Why? Because they wanted to know what was going on in the literary gatherings and debate with us and as they didn't know how to read, they had to make an effort, and they practiced and read it again until they finally learned to read after so much effort. [This was also possible] because, when reading the books for the literary gatherings, they had someone to read with at home, relatives or friends who came to visit and helped them to read. (Student)

The *dialogic reading* that occurs in these schools allows children to learn to help others, collaborate, explain things to one another, express their ideas, consider others' views, encourage one another, engage in dialogue, etc. Communication skills, vocabulary and reading are all substantially improved in these sessions, and the activities develop solidarity and friendly relationships within the group. All of these achievements make the students love reading and want to read more.

> Another thing that the literary gatherings are achieving is that you really want to read, you want to read more books. One example is a girl from my class called Janna who started to read more books thanks to the literary gatherings. (Student)

The gatherings are based on reading classics of world literature, which is a key aspect of the success of this SEA. *The Odyssey*, *Don Quixote*, the *Thousand and One Nights* and *The Aeneid* are only some examples of the types of books that children read for the *dialogic literary gatherings*. As Marta explained, she and her classmates engage in deep debates because they read these books, which address important topics that have always been important to human beings. They debate the situations experienced by the characters, the values and conflicts that are reflected in the book, and this activity causes them to compare these situations with their own lives and content from other curricular areas:

In the gatherings we talk about things that happen to us: love, fidelity, wisdom… We have already read several books, and we compare the characters (…) In the literary gatherings, we debate what happens to us and relate it to the books. Very important debate topics have come up, such as: fidelity, love, and feelings, the "cool" ones, religions, friendship, braveness, prudence… Well, very important issues. (Student)

In the same process, pupils improve their reading and overall language skills and reflect on profound topics related to life that do not often emerge in regular classroom interaction but benefit social relationships inside and outside the classroom and school. In this vein, Marta concluded her remarks at the European Parliament as follows:

To finish, I would like to share a sentence that one of the girls from my class said and that we liked very much and we still remember. It is about the book Don Quixote. To become a knight, Don Quixote needed a horse, armor, a name and a place and… a lady to love. He found Dulcinea del Toboso. My classmate chose this idea because she said she liked it very much. And when the teacher asked, 'why do you like this idea so much?', she said: 'Because if we don't love we feel alone'. (Student)

The audience, amazed by what had just happened, gave Marta a tremendous round of applause. A member of the European Parliament, seated next to Marta, looked on this 10-year-old girl with admiration. He spoke next and congratulated her with the following words: *Well, after this speech…* The audience was laughing with complicity because after that speech, who would dare to speak? He continued:

I think it has probably been one of the best speeches I have ever heard in this house since 2004. Congratulations Marta! And sometimes I think, it's for politicians to shut up and listen, especially when they hear these kinds of speeches… if you are that good at the age of ten… Goodness! At twenty, you are going to be running this place!

The Successful Educational Actions explained in this chapter, which are based on effective ways to group students and allocate human resources, all improved students' learning and achievement in the schools where they were implemented. Based on this evidence of favorable results, these SEAs have already had an impact at the political level. These findings from the INCLUD-ED project were reflected in two resolutions of the European Parliament addressing the education of children with minority and migratory backgrounds, with a special focus on the need to avoid placing them in segregated spaces.

- The *European Parliament resolution of 2 April 2009 on educating the children of migrants* (2008/2328(*INI*)) emphasizes the need to improve measures for integration. More specifically, the Parliament "stresses the need to integrate migrants and social categories (such as Roma people) in society. Integration must be based on the principles of equal opportunities in education, ensuring equal access to quality education". It also asserted: "Any solutions—whether temporary or permanent—that are based on segregation must be rejected. Parliament also considers that, in order to improve integration into society of children of migrants, it is necessary to involve them in a wide range of extracurricular activities".

- *The European Parliament resolution of* 9 *March* 2011 *on the EU strategy on Roma inclusion* (2010/2276(*INI*)) calls on the Commission and the Member States "to combat every form of social and educational exclusion of the Roma and to encourage all programmes that invest in education for Roma people", as well as "to support initiatives which have proved effective in preventing any form of segregation and prioritise inclusive projects that promote educational success and involve the participation of Roma families".

The SEAs analyzed in this chapter are alternatives that have demonstrated potential to overcome segregation and educational inequalities. The following chapter will explain how community members can contribute to this objective and improve learning for all children when family and community participation is a core aspect of the school activity.

References

Blachowicz, C. L. Z., & Obrochta, C. (2005). Vocabulary visits: Virtual field trips for content vocabulary development. *Reading Teacher, 59*(3), 262–268.

Elboj, C., & Niemelä, R. (2010). Sub-communities of mutual learners in the classroom: The case of interactive groups. *Revista de Psicodidáctica, 15*(2), 177–189.

Gatt, S., Puigdellívol, I., & Molina, S. (2010). Mead's contributions to learners' identities. *Revista de Psicodidáctica, 15*(2), 223–238.

Merton, R. K. (1968). The Matthew effect in science. *Science, 59*, 56–63.

Merton, R. K. (1973). *The Sociology of Science*. Chicago: Chicago University Press.

Oliver, E., & Gatt, S. (2010). De los actos comunicativos de poder a los actos comunicativos dialógicos en las aulas organizadas en grupos interactivos. *Signos, 43*(2), 279–294.

Pulido, C., & Zepa, B. (2010). La interpretación interactiva de los textos a través de las tertulias literarias dialógicas. *Signos, 43*(2), 295–309.

Serrano, M. A., Mirceva, J., & Larena, R. (2010). Dialogic imagination in literacy development. *Revista de Psicodidáctica, 15*(2), 191–205.

Soler, M. (2001). *Dialogic Reading: A New Understanding of the Reading Event (Doctoral Dissertation)*. Boston: Harvard University.

Soler, M. (2003–2005). *Lectura dialógica e igualdad de género en las interacciones en el aula*. [Dialogic learning and gender equality in classroom interactions]. RTD National Plan. Spanish Ministry of Employment and Social Affairs. Women's Institute.

Soler, M. (2004). Reading to share: Accounting for others in dialogic literary gatherings. In Bertau, M. (Ed.), *Aspects of the Dialogic Self. International Cultural-Historical Human Sciences* (pp. 157–183). Berlin: Lehmanns Media.

Stanovich, K. E. (1986). Matthew effects in reading: Some consequences of individual differences in the acquisition of literacy. *Reading Research Quarterly, 21*(4), 360–407.

Tellado, I., & Sava, S. (2010). The role of non-expert adult guidance in the dialogic construction of knowledge. *Revista de Psicodidáctica, 15*(2), 163–176.

Valls, R., & Kyriakides, L. (2013). The power of Interactive groups: How diversity of adults volunteering in classroom groups can promote inclusion and success for children of vulnerable minority ethnic populations. *Cambridge Journal of Education, 43*(1), 17–33.

Wells, G., & Arauz, R. M. (2006). Dialogue in the classroom. *Journal of the Learning ciences,* *15*(3), 379–428.
Wells, G. (1989). Language in the classroom: Literacy and collaborative talk. *Language and Education,* *3*(4), 251–273.

Chapter 5
Successful Educational Actions Through Family Involvement

Family involvement in educational activities is proven to improve children's academic outcomes. In this sense, the results obtained by INCLUD-ED highlighted five types of family/community involvement, i.e., informative, consultative, decisive, evaluative and educative, and their individual effects on academic achievement. The results indicate that the decisive, evaluative and educative types contribute the most to academic success. Examples of successful actions involving families are the *dialogic literary gatherings* (non-academic interactions where families are involved in reading classic literature), family digital and media literacy and parents and children's clubs. The research reveals a connection between the aforementioned types of family involvement and student learning outcomes, as such family and community involvement in education transforms educational interactions in the school, the street and the household.

A large body of literature indicates that family and community involvement in schools enhances student achievement and general well-being at school (Backer et al. 1997; Edwards and Warin 1999; Senechal and LeFevre 2002). Community participation is especially important for students from minority cultures, as it contributes to greater coordination between in-home and school activities (Boscardin and Jacobson 1996; Beckman et al. 1998; Aubert and Valls 2003; Gómez and Vargas 2003; Driessen et al. 2005; Ringold et al. 2005).

Throughout our analysis of educational systems and review of the existing literature, we identified five types of community participation in schools (Table 5.1), which differ in the form and degree of family and community members' participation and involvement: *informative, consultative, decisive, evaluative*, and *educative participation*. The INCLUD-ED project also found that the different types of participation are related to the school outcomes observed. The following table summarizes these five types.

The research conducted during the INCLUD-ED project provided new evidence regarding which of these types of family and community involvement best contribute to improvements in academic achievement and coexistence. The results from the case studies presented here provide a better understanding of the ways in which family and community participation contribute to school success and social cohesion and how that participation is operationalized in successful European schools.

© The Author(s) 2015
R. Flecha (Ed.), INCLUD-ED Consortium, *Successful Educational Actions for Inclusion and Social Cohesion in Europe*, SpringerBriefs in Education,
DOI 10.1007/978-3-319-11176-6_5

Table 5.1 Five types of family and community participation in schools

Types of family and community participation	
1. Informative	Parents are informed about school activities, school operations, and decisions that have been made
	Parents do not participate in making these decisions. A common form of informative participation is a general parents' meeting
2. Consultative	Parents have a limited impact on decision making
	Their participation is based on consultation
	They participate through the school's statutory bodies
3. Decisive	Community members participate in decision-making processes by becoming representatives in decision-making bodies
	Family and community members monitor the school's accountability in terms of its educational results
4. Evaluative	Family and community members participate in pupils' learning processes by helping evaluate the children's school progress
	Family and community members participate in the assessment of school programs and the curriculum
5. Educative	Family and community members participate in pupils' learning activities, both during regular school hours and after school
	Family and community members participate in educational programs that respond to their needs

We conducted six longitudinal case studies in five EU countries (Malta, Finland, Lithuania, the UK and Spain) in schools with low-SES families and strong community involvement where students exhibited greater educational progress relative to schools with similar characteristics. While many studies have identified the link between school success and community involvement Sheldon and Sanders (2009), INCLUD-ED explored this link in greater depth. The types of family and community participation identified in this research were found to have a direct or indirect impact on academic and non-academic success. A direct impact means that participation in these successful actions per se resulted in improved academic performance and behavior. In other cases, the actions led to changes in the person or situations involved, which then influenced the children's academic achievement or improved non-academic aspects of the educational process.

> After studying these cases in depth for 4 years, the evidence revealed that the *decisive, evaluative,* and *educative* types of participation contribute the most to pupils' academic success.

Based on a cross-case analysis of the six cases considered, we identified three types of family and community participation that made demonstrated contributions to school success and social cohesion. These types are: participation in family education, participation in decision-making processes and evaluation, and participation in classrooms and learning spaces. An annual, case-by-case analysis (2006–2010) allowed us to identify the Successful Educational Actions each school implemented to involve families and communities in the school. Moreover, each school, implemented these measures in a specific manner and adapted them to the particular characteristics of the context, and thus, there are also certain features that make these forms of participation unique to each school.

Additionally, these types of participation, which are open to all members of the community (Oliver et al. 2009), contradict the notion that schools are places where social inequalities are reproduced and perpetuated and promote the image of schools as spaces for social transformation and overcoming inequality. The schools studied are examples of this transformative capacity, and the actions analyzed are components that can help to increase the transformative capacity of other schools across Europe.

In the following section, we explain the three successful types of family and community participation and the benefits they produce.

5.1 Family Involvement in Learning Activities

This type of family and community participation proved to have the greatest positive impact on children's learning outcomes. Family and community involvement in educational activities includes adults' participation both in children's learning processes and their own learning as adults.

When pupils' relatives and other community members participate in the children's classrooms and other learning spaces, the classroom teacher is better able to attend to the needs of all children; this improves both learning by individual students and the general experience of harmony in the classroom. In addition, children have more, and different, opportunities for interaction with adults.

The case studies demonstrated that a range of specific activities makes these changes possible. For instance, in many of the studied schools, family members and volunteers participated in the SEAs described above; these are implemented in spaces inside and outside the classroom where pupils learn curricular content. Examples include: *interactive groups*, individual support inside the classroom, homework clubs, after-school writing programs, and literary gatherings with children. Adult participation in all of these spaces made it possible to increase the number and diversity of interactions available to all children, which in turn accelerated the learning process.

> Family and community participation in the classroom involves the effective reallocation of existing human resources in the community, specifically by employing them in the classroom to support student learning.

In the case of schools with migrants and cultural minority groups, their involvement in the school is important, particularly the participation of women. The evidence collected helps to dispel potential stereotypes related to the low participation of specific groups in schools, such as the stereotypes applied to Arab women. As confirmed by an educational official, Arab Muslim women are one of the most involved groups:

> And the ones who are the life and soul of the school, participate the most readily and are the most involved are minority groups such as Moroccan mothers, who are highly involved, and I think that should be valued. Few schools in Terrassa [the city where the school is located] have really managed to get the mothers from these minority groups involved. (Educational official)

Patricia, the immigrant mother from Colombia mentioned above, explained that all of the families in her school participate in the classroom whenever they can, and the school takes advantage of their participation to improve the learning opportunities of all students. For instance, the school has been able to rely on Latin American and Arab mothers who teach English in the classroom, as well as on an autochthonous retired woman who helps first year students improve their reading skills in Catalan language classes:

> What we do is that when a mother from one of the families has time, she comes, she goes into a classroom, she reads the children a story, she helps them, she reinforces their learning; there is always an assistant or a mother who is there helping the teacher, not every day but it does happen when the parents have time, for example I say, "well, look tomorrow I have time, tomorrow I'll come and I will read them a story from my country". And the same is true of all the parents. (Mother)

Moreover, the participation of non-academic women and individuals from different cultures in children's academic activities helps to overcome cultural and gender stereotypes (Christou and Puigvert 2011), as children are performing better as a result of these individuals' involvement in the classroom and other learning spaces. Thus, new cultural referents are introduced in the schools, transforming these learning environments, the socio-cultural context and increasing feelings of social cohesion in the classroom and beyond. The students value the assistance and participation of these mothers. Alicia, an autochthonous mother of two children, describes the transformation of the students' perceptions of the mothers as a result of involvement in learning activities in the classroom:

> [And in order to learn would it help them to see their mother or see you? Do you think that it would change the image they have of you as a woman?]

> Yes, yes. They see you as a mother and that is it. The woman and the mother, the wife and the mother, and of course if they see you coming out of that [role], they value you more. When their little friend or whatever says, "look your mum teaches me so well or she is so good at reading that to me or she's so good at... I don't know" above all they value it very much when their friends speak well of you, which does not happen with everyone. (Mother)

Promoting women's participation in schools (including students' relatives and other members of the community) not only makes it possible to increase the number and diversity of personal resources available to help students learn but also contributes in important ways to preventing issues related to gender violence in schools (Oliver et al. 2009). This is how the head teacher of one school described this matter:

> There were stories of some boys who were harassing some girls. The mothers came along to tell me about this situation because their daughters had told them about it, (…) then they came along to the extracurricular activities themselves because it was those boys who went along to extracurricular classes and they worked on it with them, that is [they asked them] why they were doing it, why they were lifting up the girls skirts, and said that they did not have the right to lift up their skirts. And [such behavior] was reduced, it was not eradicated but it was reduced. (Head teacher)

The inclusion of families in the classroom improves social cohesion and the classroom climate. The students improve their behavior and concentrate on learning activities when family members are present. Both family members and teachers have identified this improvement. One school had serious coexistence problems in some classrooms before the SEAs were implemented; since the families began participating, these problems are being overcome, and a positive family climate is being created. One example is Emilia, an illiterate mother, who helps to improve student behavior when she enters the classroom.

> Before I came, they were making such a racket. And one of the little girls said, "Juan's mummy is here" and they sat down. (…) and all of the kids sat there to do what the teacher said and everything went well, and the teacher was there with them [and she said,] "if I didn't see this with my own eyes I wouldn't believe it", and she also said, "when are you coming next Emilia?" (Mother)

The students confirm that if families participate in the classrooms, they behave better. Miguel, a Roma child, thinks that the children would behave much better if there was a family member in the classroom, as they would be embarrassed when forced to confront this other adult. The following is a statement from the student that confirms this improvement.

> I would also behave myself. (…) Because I would be embarrassed. (…) Well, for example, if you're having a fight with someone, that man would be flipping out. (…) Well [I would suggest] that if his mother were there, if he misbehaves, then he would behave better. (Roma child)

In a similar vein, a Roma girl called Ana admitted that children behave better when families are in the classroom helping the teachers:

> We [behave] well because we want to show them that we are good. (Roma girl)

Nuria, a teacher, agreed with Ana and described that learning in collaboration with their families is more meaningful for the children. They also respect their classmates more and wish to demonstrate that they know more and are well-behaved:

> When sometimes, as has occasionally happened, well the kids, are…they grow up, with more of a desire to work, [they say] look mum, look at me reading this, look at me working; they are more respectful, and they are proud that their classmates can see that their mother or father is there working, in some cases. (Teacher)

In addition to improving the classroom climate, the families and volunteers who participate in learning activities contribute to ensuring that all students are engaged in the learning activity and can progress in their learning. The schools analyzed have diverse students in their classrooms who are immigrants or from cultural minorities, as demonstrated previously. One teacher alone in the classroom cannot fully respond to the diversity in the classroom, and it is therefore difficult for all of the pupils to acquire the skills that are necessary and achieve good results. When more numerous and diverse adults are included in the classroom, as in the described cases, the students have the opportunity for interactions that help them to remain on task when solving a problem and acquire the skills and knowledge that will allow them to succeed academically (Flecha and Soler 2013).

The participation of volunteers in the classroom reinforces the learning of the students who face the greatest learning difficulties. Laura, a head teacher who directly participates in organizing the volunteers at her school, explained that the teachers observed an improvement among the most disadvantaged children as a result of having volunteers work with them. These volunteers' contribution is not to teach these students, but rather to help them remain focused on the learning activity and motivate them:

> That person comes in during the class, and helps the children, especially the ones who find it most difficult to generate a routine which works well, and in the end, all of the teachers who have had the possibility and the opportunity to have someone to help them along these lines have noticed that the students have improved their learning a great deal; we can see that it has been strengthened. (Head teacher)

Volunteer participation, for instance, allows Naima, a Moroccan girl, to perform well in a country where Moroccan students often do not succeed but instead tend to be marginalized by the educational system. Naima is aware that she can learn more thanks to the support she receives from volunteers in her school and deeply values the help she receives from them.

Other actions have been identified that include family and community involvement in children's learning activities and are improving children's learning outcomes. Examples of such improvement include *Friday Morning Coffee* (UK), a time when families come to school to be with their sons and daughters, or in *Stay and Play Peers Early Education Partnerships* (PEEPS, UK), which promotes interaction between cultural groups, or the *Writing skills* sessions (Malta), where children are given support to improve their writing and reading skills.

These opportunities to share learning activities not only transform children's realities and learning prospects but also transform the realities of family members. Their participation in these curricular and extracurricular activities allows relatives and pupils to engage in a shared learning process; as a result, both families and children engage in more academic interactions. The new educational content these activities contribute to family-child interactions increases student motivation and transforms everyone's personal relationships and lives. Ultimately, involving adults from the students' families and/or communities in learning activities provides numerous mutual benefits: both children and adults learn and share in this learning, educational interactions at school and in the home are coordinated, new school-related interactions between relatives and children emerge, and all of these outcomes increase the opportunities for everyone involved to further their learning.

5.2 Family Education: Dialogic Literary Gatherings

INCLUD-ED has documented family and community education initiatives in several successful school programmes, such as the *learning communities* in Spain and the Lifelong Learning Centres in Malta. These programmes focus on promoting basic education among family members, in addition to other adult educational and cultural activities. The various successful schools that the project studied implemented various forms of family education. Some examples are:

- Courses on literacy, numeracy, ICT, and other topics were given priority based on the parents' knowledge gaps. These were found in all 6 of the schools studied.
- Talks based on areas of interest to the community. These were also observed in all the schools considered.
- Learning spaces shared by children and families. These were found in Malta (After School Club), the UK (the AMBER and SOFIE projects) and Finland (Parent's evening, with interpreters).
- *Dialogic literary gatherings*, in which family members read and discuss classic works of literature. These were only found in Spain.

A crucial characteristic of successful forms of family and community education is that the activities are organized in response to the needs and requests of families. Many activities are designed with and for mothers, to create spaces where they feel comfortable speaking openly.

In the case studies where *dialogic literary gatherings* were observed, multiple pieces of evidence were obtained regarding how *dialogic reading* in family and community education contributes to the transformation of the interactions between families and their children, all of which accelerate learning, and promote personal and social transformations. In Chap. 4, we explained how the *dialogic literary gatherings* are conducted and the impact they have on the children's learning. In what follows, we will explain how the gatherings are organized in the schools with mothers, fathers and other community members. During these sessions, adult participants participate in reading classic works of literature, including writers such as Kafka, Joyce, Dostoyevsky, García Lorca, and Cervantes. By engaging in dialogue about the literature, participants deepen their understanding of language and engage in debates based on their own life experiences. The debates are based on egalitarian dialogue (Flecha 2000); that is, all contributions are valued based on the arguments provided, irrespective of whether the speaker is an academic, lacks formal education or is of migrant origin and is not proficient in the language of the host country. The dialogues and reflections concern topics of universal importance precisely

Fig. 5.1 In the *dialogic
literary gatherings* adults
readand engage in debate
aboutclassic works of
literature

because the books are classic works of literature. For these two reasons, the *dialogic
literary gatherings* are a very empowering experience. The families that participate
in the gatherings tend to be the most involved in other learning and decision spaces.

The *dialogic literary gatherings* with adults are a space that is open to participation by families and the community and affect adults' educative and cultural
backgrounds and children's learning. We observed that when schools employ this
type of family education activity, children acquire more of the basic skills offered in
the curriculum; in addition, absenteeism declines and more children register for
school. Further, the literary gatherings, and the family literacy and language
courses, help to transform family relationships, increasing the confidence of parents
with little formal education and transforming at-home interactions, as parents and
children engage in dialogue about the books they are reading and other issues at
school. For instance, one school developed such an activity that involved children
and their mothers, many of them immigrants. The result is that in families that never
read books in the home, the parents and children now discuss Homer's *Odyssey*
over dinner. A climate is created in the homes in which books, reading and discussions on the topics of classic works of literature are present in students' daily
lives, and these experiences affect their motivation to read and improve their lin-
guistic skills. Therefore, we observed an increase in the number and types of
academic interactions in the home. Furthermore, when analyzing our data, we
found evidence that relatives became better able to understand the schoolwork their
children were engaged in and were thus empowered to help them with their
homework (Fig. 5.1).

The overall analysis demonstrates that family and community members' participation in educational activities or family education improves children's academic
results. This improvement can not only be observed in the improved acquisition of
the basic competencies included in the curriculum but also in positive effects on
other aspects, such as reduced absenteeism and increased enrolment. These findings
are particularly relevant for the cases studied in Spain and the UK, which provided
insights into the different mechanisms that promote this improvement.

Family education helps to align educational practices in school with those at home. Family and community education helps families to convey a positive attitude towards learning, which is then reflected in the students' improved attitude toward learning and increased motivation to learn inside and outside the classroom.

> The results obtained by INCLUD-ED demonstrate that we need not wait for the next generation to reverse the trends of children failing in school and leaving school when they are still young, as *certain types of family education can have an immediate, transformative effect on educational outcomes.*

Family training also increases families' academic expectations for their children. By participating in family education, parents begin to understand the education system and realize that they can learn and interact with other social referents, and thus become aware that their children can also succeed in the educational system. This translates into higher expectations for their children's learning potential. Moreover, having children observe their parents engaging in educational activities similar to their own improves their relationships with their parents.

According to the research literature, family training enables parents to assist in their children's learning process. Based on the evidence collected during this project, democratically designed family training makes it possible to improve parental education levels. As a result, family education allows families to increase their skills in terms of reading, writing and discussing school issues with their children, and hence, it promotes increased academic interactions between children and their families. These findings are supported by the conclusions of previous works arguing that improving parents' reading skills provides low-income parents with the opportunity to align themselves with the school culture. This justifies the emphasis placed on the need to ensure equity in the distribution of literacy programs.

In sum, the case studies analyzed demonstrated that participation serves to empower parents, who can help promote further educational development among their children and greater social cohesion. Many researchers make statistical inferences based on responses to international surveys and conclude that there is an association between children's school performance and parental education levels and/or number of books in the home, and analysts draw on those correlations to support arguments for investing in human capital. This falls far from what research in learning and development through interaction has supported. Low familial educational levels only have a major influence when Successful Educational Actions are not implemented. We need not wait for a generation of parents with university degrees to ensure that their children succeed at school, for example, if schools offer family education for those parents.

5.3 Participation in School Evaluations and Decision-Making

Participation in decision-making and in school evaluations is the third type of successful family and community participation. Throughout the case studies, we observed interventions designed to involve more representatives of the different groups in decision-making, thus implementing a form of democratic participation. This type of organization includes the voices of all participants in managing the center and draws on the notion of "cultural intelligence" (Flecha 2000). Families and other members of the community actively participate in decision-making processes; in cooperation with teachers, they make decisions on issues related to learning, the organization of the school, and/or ways to resolve and prevent conflicts and organize school activities. As a result of this approach, the value assigned to individual contributions is not based on the academic or socio-economic status of the individuals, but rather on the arguments and contributions they provide; these arguments may come from either a more academic or a more practical direction.

In some of the schools, we observed the use of *mixed committees* as a decision-making body. These committees comprise members of all groups in the community: families, teachers, pupils, and other community representatives, who meet to decide on core aspects of school operations, from improving infrastructure to organizing the supports students require to succeed at school. Relying on mixed committees for decision-making implies that the school professionals have high expectations regarding the family members' ability to contribute to managing the center and not simply participating in peripheral activities (Díez et al. 2011). To promote participation in the mixed committees, an agreement is made: all voices will be considered and all committee members are equally important. The use of mixed committees to manage the school has increased the involvement of family members, as their opinions are considered equally valid as those of the teaching staff. Our research identified a connection between this type of participation and improvements in students' academic results.

Jaime, a teacher who had worked at one of the primary schools we studied for 20 years, realized the importance of these participatory spaces with respect to children's academic success. He supported the notion that the families that participate the most in decision-making processes experienced decreased absenteeism among their children. He particularly observed this change among Arab families, which are an important part of the school population:

> The children of the people who participate are the ones who rarely miss school, that is, it is clearly a result of the involvement of the mother or the father; it is usually mothers who come along the most, I suppose (…) due to the fact that the fathers work. Above all Arab families, really [they are] the ones you see who participate the most, you can see that those children are more motivated, there is greater motivation, they come to school more. (Teacher)

Jaime also linked this type of family participation to children finding increased meaning in school life and work. Reducing absenteeism and increasing the motivation to learn has led, according to teachers such as Jaime, to increased learning levels among all pupils:

> It has an impact on their motivation, and when the children are more motivated, then logically, learning levels improve. (Teacher)

Lola is a Roma woman who works in the child and youth center in the neighborhood. She completely agreed that this link between the involvement of families in decision-making processes and students being more motivated to do homework and participate in activities exists:

> I do think that they are more productive, that the children see their father, they are more motivated, and do things like that, I think that it will be better for them, I think that it contributes more to them, they are more motivated at school, I think so anyway. (Roma community member)

The *Families' Assembly* is another well-established procedure to enable broad participation by the families of all students. This assembly was established to assess the overall operations of the school and make decisions on important issues, such as how to organize classroom interactions and address the increasing numbers of immigrant children attending the school. Families from diverse cultural backgrounds and with various levels of education (even some with no formal education), along with teachers and volunteers, agreed to implement educational actions that would best respond to the students' educational needs and requests. Two decisions were made as a result of this assembly. First, all pupils would remain in their classrooms and would not be separated into different classrooms according to their learning levels. Second, all available resources and support would be applied in the regular classroom; these include support teachers for children with special needs, along with volunteers and family members. *Interactive groups* was one action implemented that responded to such criteria and addressed the students' diversity while improving everyone's learning. This was possible, first, because family members participated in deciding how to improve their children's learning and, second, because of their participation in the *interactive groups* as volunteers.

Interactions among community members in meetings such as the Families' Assembly or the mixed committees provide mutual benefits because all of the participants—families, other community members and professionals—share diverse knowledge. One consequence of such interactions is that individuals dismantle their prejudices, and as a result, the general sense of harmony and coexistence in the community improves. For this to occur, the meetings must not be merely consultative or informative; they are primarily spaces for decision-making. Thus, schedules need to be flexible and account for the needs of families and the community. Broad-based participation in these spaces promotes both transparency and improved adjustments to the prevailing community conditions.

To achieve this purpose, the meeting times are arranged in a flexible manner. Therefore, by offering a variety of meeting times, individuals who would otherwise not be able to, are about to enjoy greater opportunities to participate. As a consequence, families feel that the school is taking their needs and problems into consideration, and the school can take advantage of all the diverse contributions of more community members. Laura, a head teacher, explained the importance of establishing flexible timetables for the meetings to adapt to the needs and characteristics of families; for instance, while the best time for most of the mothers to meet was in the afternoon while their children where in class, the fathers were working at that time and could never come, and therefore, another meeting was arranged for them in the evening.

> The school keeps an eye on that a lot and sometimes will hold the same meeting twice, once for those mothers who can make it once for the fathers to come too, why not? Because, for example, in the Roma population or the Arab population, it's normally the women who come to the school, and therefore the school really tries to get the men to come, and therefore get them to participate just as much as the women. We try to do that a lot, and most of the time there are twice as many meetings for that reason. The important participatory meetings are doubled for that particular reason. The year when they did the dream phase again, they held two meetings, one with mothers from 3 to 5 and one more with the fathers at 10 o'clock at night, so that the fathers could also talk about their dreams. (Head teacher)

Parental participation in decision-making processes is especially important in multicultural contexts. Due to the presence of different cultural groups and immigrants, a lack of knowledge of the language could be a barrier for these parents to participate in the school. Faced with this barrier, actions such as the presence of a translator at the meetings can be employed to ensure that minority groups are also represented and can participate equally:

> [And, for example, do you think immigrant families participate equally?] Yes. [And the issue of language is not a problem?] Because there is a translator. [Is there a translator at the meetings?] Yes. [And do you see Moroccan or South American people, for example, participating?] Yes. It's equal, yes. (Local government employee involved in the school)

Another example of minority families participating in decision-making is the *Parents' evenings with interpreters*, held in Finland. The aim of this program is to include the voices of families that have found it more difficult to participate in the school. The objective of these meetings is to gather the families' requests, concerns, and needs. The teachers and family members engage in a conversation, which includes the families' proposals. The process creates an egalitarian relationship between teachers and families. To encourage participation by these families, this school provides translations into several languages. Moreover, meetings are scheduled at times that consider the participants' working hours and make it possible for them to attend.

The democratic organization of the center based on actions such as that described above affects the relationship between teachers and pupils. In our analysis of the case studies, we found that when schools consider the contributions of everyone involved in running the school, it becomes possible for individuals to share ideas and contribute on an equal level, irrespective of their role in the school. Thus it allows everyone involved determining better responses to concerns that are raised. Coexistence and collaboration also improve: from the moment when community members begin to participate in the process of designing common norms, everyone experiences a greater sense of shared responsibility to manage the school and address the school's needs. Therefore, one consequence of this process is that active participation in decision-making makes education more meaningful for everyone in the community.

The children have had to alter their perceptions to understand that the school is composed of all the social agents in the neighborhood. Therefore, involving families and community members in decision-making processes allows the school to become part of the neighborhood and not merely an addition to it. Moreover, this involvement promotes the understanding of the school as a neighborhood space where everyone is involved and where the children's education is the most important issue. Aleix, a member of the Educational Psychology Assessment Team associated with one of the schools, observed the following in the children:

> But for the kids the fact of knowing that many of the decisions were made with the participation of parents is also a way to understand the school and understand that it is not something which is external to them, that everyone participates, that there is very strong involvement by their families, and whether you want them to or not, they place a great deal of importance on education which they would not have otherwise. (Member of the Educational Psychology Assessment Team)

Being involved in decision-making processes produces a feeling of belonging to the school community and respect for these processes. In another school studied, families participate in decision-making related to the rules of coexistence and the prevention and resolution of conflicts. This involvement has produced important benefits. During the first observations conducted on the playground at the beginning of the 2006–2007 school year, it was necessary to have 8 adults, including teachers, mediators and other individuals from community organizations to control conflicts. The involvement of the families and the community as a whole in the creation of school rules and the consequences for violating those rules improved coexistence in the school. At the end of the same school year, it was only necessary to have 3 teachers on the school playground (to gather observations). The entire school community participated in the creation of a Constitution for the school. This democratic activity provided an incentive for the participation of families and neighborhood organizations. This means that the entire community respects these rules and statements: children, families, social professionals, teachers, etc. Araceli, a teacher from this school, reflected on this concept:

> Well, yes, since everyone knows about it and has participated in it, they make it their own. Therefore, they respect it a lot more because they have done it; we have all done it together. (Teacher)

Traditionally, professional educators have been responsible for evaluating student progress and designing curricula. Participation in evaluations is based on the premise that all educational agents in a community wish to see their children succeed at school. When families and community members are included in the evaluation or curriculum design process, they can share knowledge and strategies, enhance the effectiveness of the actions taken to improve learning, and increase the potential to improve children's learning conditions.

The participation of families in evaluating and planning the curriculum has been identified as important in preschool education to ensure that children succeed in learning core subjects. The *Individual Education Plan* and the *Individual Early Childhood and Education Plan*, both developed in Finland, are examples of this. They draw on the notion that collaboration between different educational agents makes it possible to prevent learning difficulties at an early stage. Through this partnership, pupils feel supported and have more self-esteem and higher expectations of their ability to learn. Moreover, in general terms, this approach helps to prevent learning difficulties from becoming serious problems.

In this approach, pupils with disabilities benefit when teachers and families collaborate in designing the curriculum, as the two have direct and complementary knowledge of the pupils and the attention they need. This allows the collaborators to individualize the curriculum in a more inclusive way, and thereby better accelerate student learning. This type of collaboration also promotes high expectations for these pupils, which has a positive impact on their self-esteem. To allow and encourage family and community participation in curriculum development and evaluation processes, egalitarian and collaborative relationships must be established with the school staff to ensure that families and community members can make real contributions that have an impact on the children's learning process.

The "Dialogic Report" was a strategy that one school adopted to involve families, organizations and associations from the neighborhood in the school's annual evaluations. This school included the voices of the community as a whole in the official annual evaluation document, which must be submitted by all state schools. The following is a quotation from the document:

> The report is an internal evaluation of what has been planned, taking into account that our programming was quite general and based on the general principles of *learning communities*. This report was written dialogically by all of the Associations [Asociación Calí, Secretariado Gitano, Social Services and persons who participated in the project, family members, volunteers, external advisors from CEP -teachers' center-, Ctroadi -territorial resource center for guidance, diversity and interculturality- and the Education Delegation], both externally and internally. All of these conclusions were gathered together and captured in this report, and this will be the starting point for the creation of the PGA [General Annual Program] for the next school year. (La Paz School 2006–2007: 2)

The dialogic evaluation conducted in the school based on the Dialogic Report described above, along with all of the organizations and community members, was used to coordinate and extend the educational provision in the school and the neighborhood. For example, this evaluation identified a number of overlapping extracurricular activities and the inability of certain stakeholders to attend meetings due to their work schedules. In response, the school elected to hold these meetings at two different times of the day to ensure that individuals who cannot attend one meeting could attend the other. Moreover, while parents do not have substantial input regarding the core curricular activities in the school, they have been given space to evaluate other, less formal aspects such as extra-curricular activities, which also serve as opportunities for student learning (Table 5.2).

Table 5.2 Characteristics of educative, decisive and evaluative participation and improvements achieved

Educative participation	
Family and community participation in learning activities	
(a) Family and community education	
Education activities organized according to the demands of the families	Increased acquisition of basic competences
	Reduced absenteeism
	Make in-school educational practices similar to those in the home
	Increased family expectations of students
	Improving the educational levels of parents and relatives
(b) Participation in classrooms and the children's other learning spaces	
More effective reallocation of the existing human resources in the community	Community participation supports children learning core subjects
Participation in extracurricular learning activities help to ensure that pupils can catch up to the learning level of their peers	Promotes interaction among pupils
	Increases supportive interactions among children and between children and adults, and this accelerates the learning process
	Increases pupils' motivation
	Improves multicultural coexistence
	The participation of volunteers and relatives in the education centers extends learning time beyond the school day
Decisive participation	
Family and community participation in decision-making processes	
Includes everyone's voices in the management of the center	Overcomes prejudices and improves coexistence
The meetings are not merely consultative or informative	Enhances the relationship between teachers and students
To encourage the participation of all community members, translation into several languages is provided	Becomes a means of creating a shared meaning of education for the entire community
	Reduces absenteeism
	Increases children's motivation to learn
Evaluative participation	
Family and community participation in school evaluations and the curriculum	
Families and community members are included in the evaluation or curriculum design process	Increases opportunities for improving children's learning conditions

(continued)

Table 5.2 (continued)

Evaluative participation	
Evaluation is shared among parents and professionals	Makes it possible to design and better adapt learning experiences to the pupils' needs, and thus learning is improved and accelerated
The community helps teachers to identify aspects in which pupils need to devote additional effort	Increases self-esteem and expectations regarding students' ability to learn
	Learning difficulties are prevented
	The curriculum is individualized in more inclusive ways

The participation and involvement of family and community members in the school entails transformational processes that transcend the school itself and reach other social spheres that affect the lives of the participants. These transformations occur in the neighborhood and concern housing, health, employment, social and political participation and community members' personal lives.

One of the challenges related to *housing* is access to information. As schools are becoming spaces for multiple interactions, the opportunities to access different types of information increase thereby the problem of information provision related to housing. The analysis of the different case studies demonstrates that providing access to housing information and improving the community network increase opportunities for community members to enjoy improved housing conditions. In these spaces, and through different interactions, information related to economic issues, banking transactions, neighborhood rules or specific rules in a building and housing opportunities are discussed and help to improve housing conditions. Moreover, the housing dimension is also related to architectural demands and urban reforms intended to foster a safe, communitarian space.

In the contexts in which the schools we analyzed are located, which are sometimes very deprived areas, schools become a source of safety by providing safe spaces for residents where they can spend their leisure time. In these contexts the schools have developed initiatives to create welcoming and safe spaces in the neighborhood surrounding the school. As a result of these efforts, community participation and coordination have transcended the walls of the school to improve the living conditions and physical environment of the neighborhood.

There is growing evidence suggesting that the income distribution, in addition to the overall standard of living of the different members of society, is a key determinant of the population's *health*. Community involvement is a promising strategy to improve community health. Our case studies reveal that family and community participation increases the participants' sense of empowerment and contributes to overcoming barriers that individuals, families and the overall community face when attempting to secure good overall health (Flecha et al. 2011).

For migrants, language learning promotes integration into a community and helps them to understand how health services operate. Thus, promoting local language learning improves health conditions. Furthermore, it provides general skills, values, and dispositions that offer members of the public greater opportunities (access to the information, solidarity networks, and empowerment) to adopt attitudes associated with caring for their personal health and that of the family. In particular, there is evidence that investments in education and literacy, especially those addressed to women, can reduce the incidence of health problems. When the migrant population is able to learn the local language, they enjoy greater autonomy in understanding the information they receive from health services. This was noted in the case studies conducted in Spain and the UK, where migrants highlighted, for example, that learning the local language allows them to access health services without being accompanied by a relative; they feel confident that they can go alone. Additionally, and as a consequence of increased access to health information (services and health conditions), in some cases the school and/or other community organizations have taken the initiative to promote and support health services in schools.

Exclusion from social services can lead to social problems such as alcohol consumption, smoking (Laaksonen et al. 1999), and drug abuse. Therefore, health is an aspect of social life that contributes to social cohesion within a community. Promoting healthful habits in the community can contribute to the development of social cohesion. In the schools we analyzed, we observed instances in which the actions of the schools had a direct impact on improving the health status of children, their families, and the community, thereby contributing to the transformation of the neighborhood.

Family education activities increase the *work* opportunities of these families, as was noted in the case studies. First, these efforts succeed because the skills and competences of the family members improve and they enrich their educational background. Second, regarding migrant community members, family education is an opportunity to learn the language of the host country, and this in turn, improves their participation in the labor market. As a consequence, investing in family education strengthens the connection between education and labor opportunities.

Moreover, volunteering experience is occasionally valued in the labor market, increasing individuals' professional experience and helping them discover better work opportunities. Finally, community participation in the school allows for the development of a number of interactive spaces that provide participants with access to an information network, thus overcoming social isolation and discrimination in the search for a job. In this respect, the schools become places where networks are created and strengthened and where information on job vacancies is more accessible.

Additionally, in some cases, community members indicated that their participation in the school delivered new employment opportunities for themselves or their families, for example by temporarily employing some of the pupils' relatives in the renovation of the school building. In this sense, both the school and the family members benefited from the involvement of family and community members in the school.

By developing various activities in conjunction with families and students and continuously transforming and improving the school in a way that can be perceived by the participants, family and community participation increases and is extended to other areas and activities. Nonetheless, certain conditions have been identified that must be promoted to improve such participation. These concern egalitarian dialogue, cultural intelligence, the democratic organization of the school, and adjusting schedules, spaces and topics to the realities of the participants to better meet their needs.

Participation in the school has a multiplicative effect that transcends the school itself and influences participation in other community spaces to transform the neighborhood. As a result of committed central involvement in the school, the community becomes more involved in improving their environment beyond the school's walls and more engaged in demanding better facilities to improve their neighborhood.

References

Aubert, A., & Valls, R. (2003). Dones Gitanes que superen l'exclusió social a través de l'educació. *Educació Social-Revista d'Intervenció Socioeducativa, 24*, 22–32.

Backer, L., Scher, D., & Mackler, K. (1997). Home and family influences on motivations for literacy. *Educational Psychologist, 32*, 69–82.

Beckman, P. J., Barnwell, D., Horn, E., Hanson, M. J., Gutierrez, S., & Lieber, J. (1998). Communities, families, and inclusion. *Early Childhood Research Quarterly, 13*(1), 125–150.

Boscardin, M. L., & Jacobson, S. (1996). The inclusive school, integrating diversity and solidarity through community-based management. *Journal of Educational Administration, 35*(5), 466–476.

Christou, M., & Puigvert, L. (2011). The role of "other women" in current educational transformations. *International Studies in Sociology of Education, 21*(1), 77–90.

Díez, D., Gatt, S., & Racionero, S. (2011). Placing immigrant and minority family and community members at the school's centre: the role of community participation. *European Journal of Education, 46*(2), 184–196.

Driessen, G., Smit, F., & Sleegers, P. (2005). Parental involvement and educational achievement. *British Educational Research Journal, 31*(4), 509–532.

Edwards, A., & Warin, J. (1999). Parental involvement in raising the achievement of primary school pupils: Why bother? *Oxford Review of Education, 25*(3), 325–341.

Flecha, A., García, R., & Rudd, R. (2011). Using health literacy in school to overcome inequalities. *European Journal of Education, 46*(2), 209–218.

Flecha, R. (2000). *Sharing Words*. Lanham, M.D: Rowman & Littlefield.

Flecha, R., & Soler, M. (2013). Turning difficulties into possibilities: engaging Roma families and students in school through dialogic learning. *Cambridge Journal of Education, 43*(4), 451–465.

Gómez, J., & Vargas, J. (2003). Why Roma do not like mainstream schools: voices of a people without territory. *Harvard Educational Review, 73*(4), 559–590.

La Paz School. (2006–2007). *PGA - Annual general programme for the next school year*. Dialogic report, Spain. Albacete: La Paz School.

Laaksonen, M., McAlister, A., Laatikainen, T., & Puska, P. (1999). *Do health behaviour and psychosocial risk factors explain the European East-West gap in health status*. Helsinki, Finland: Department of Epidemiology and Health Promotion, National Public Health Institute.

Oliver, E., Soler, M., & Flecha, R. (2009). Opening schools to all (women): efforts to overcome gender violence in Spain. *British Journal of Sociology of Education, 30*(2), 207–218.

Ringold, D., Orenstein, M. A., & Wilkens, E. (2005). *Roma in an expanding Europe: Breaking the poverty cycle*. Washington, DC: The International Bank for Reconstruction and Development / The World Bank.

Senechal, M., & LeFevre, J. (2002). Parental involvement in the development of children's reading skill: A five-year longitudinal study. *Child Development, 73*(2), 445–460.

Sheldon, S. B., & Sanders, M. G. (2009). *Principals matter: A guide to school, family and community partnerships*. California: Corwin.

Chapter 6
Schools as Learning Communities

Drawing on the results of INCLUD-ED research, the European Commission and the Council of Europe have recommended considering *schools as learning communities* to reduce early school leaving and improve learning outcomes. In schools that function as a *learning community*, teachers, families, pupils, and community members work in close collaboration to implement evidence-based, successful actions in their schools. Beginning from a community dream statement, these schools decide to transform and organize traditional settings into ones that research has demonstrated are successful. Currently, there are more than 120 schools, public and private, located in wealthy and low-income areas, with different levels of diversity, and in different countries, which have gone through this transformation and are implementing the SEAs with excellent results in the academic, emotional and social development of all pupils.

6.1 Theoretical Background

The issue of community involvement in schools has attracted significant research attention. Various studies have been interested in analyzing this approach to determine what benefits could be attributed to it (Sánchez 1999; Delgado-Gaitan 2001; Epstein 2001; García 2002). According to Wells (1999), for instance, educators can transform their schools and classrooms into communities of inquirers. Lave and Wenger's (1991) framework sheds light on the analysis of local community projects and regards them as communities of practitioners. Employing the theoretical concept of legitimate peripheral participation, they provide a new approach to understanding how community involvement, education and social cohesion are connected. This connection has proven especially relevant in educational centers, which are attended by children from social groups at risk of exclusion and immigrant families (Buckingham 2005). In this process, community involvement becomes important not only for the school but also for the transformation of that community. Furthermore, community involvement in schools has

© The Author(s) 2015
R. Flecha (Ed.), INCLUD-ED Consortium, *Successful Educational Actions for Inclusion and Social Cohesion in Europe*, SpringerBriefs in Education,
DOI 10.1007/978-3-319-11176-6_6

been shown to lead to improved student performance at school (Grolnick et al. 1999; Epstein 2004; Harvard Family Research Project 2007).

Communities, of whatever type, are characterized by a number of aspects. All communities have a sense of agency; they can act, promote a sense of belonging among their members, support cohesion through commitment, and embrace diversity (Watkins 2007). Watkins (2007) describes how communities help their members to take collective action; develop connections of community members; promote collaboration; and allow for dialogue, discussion and debate to exchange ideas and opinions. Schuler (1996) regards a community as the sum of a number of dependent aspects. He identifies these as: strong democracy; education; health and well-being; economic equity, opportunity and sustainability; information and communication; and conviviality and culture.

The value and contribution of the community to the education process has been recognized in official policy documents. The 2002 No Child Left Behind (NCLB) Act in the U.S. identified, among other elements, increased parental involvement as one of the mechanisms educators should employ to improve student achievement. Schools were encouraged to create policies that valued family and community involvement, include families in decision- and policy-making processes, provide parents with information on academic content and standards, and invest in school-home initiatives. Teddie and Reynolds (2000) revealed that in low-SES areas, the trend of school failure can be reversed by implementing measures and policies based on family participation. Schools, as 'core social centers', are considered a primary means of combating social fragmentation and exclusion, as they promote and attribute a greater role to families and communities.

Epstein and Sheldon (2006) state that school, family, and community partnerships are a better strategy for locating school actions in the community than parental involvement, as these partnerships recognize that parents, educators, and other community members share the responsibility for the pupils' learning and development. This is because community involvement is a multidimensional and complex concept involving different agents acting at different levels and in different ways. Epstein and Sheldon (2006) also highlight that community partnerships are an essential component of school and classroom organization and require strong leadership. They continue to emphasize that such programs should have the goals of both better educational achievement and of obtaining equitable educational provision.

Community involvement and *learning communities* in schools have been documented to promote academic improvements in children. Improvements in literacy have been observed (Faires et al. 2000; Jordon et al. 2000) in the early years of schooling. Improving parents' reading skills provides low-income parents with a greater ability to align with the school culture (Paratore et al. 1999). This is the reason for emphasizing that governments need to ensure equity in the distribution of literacy programs (Ponzetti and Dulin 1997). The use of volunteers was also found to promote the development of reading skills among primary level pupils (Fitzgerald 2001). Progress in reading, due to community involvement programs, was also observed among older pupils at the primary level (Epstein 2001). In the case of mathematics, improvements were observed where elements of community involvement in the school were present. This was related to children's self-concepts as learners in mathematics reflecting their parents' views of them and their mathematical abilities (Frome and Eccles 1998). Parental attitudes toward science were found to play an important role in the children's interest and achievement in the subject (George and Kaplan 1998).

The research literature has also identified effects of *learning communities* on non-academic aspects. Sanders and Sheldon (2009) provide references to studies demonstrating the positive impact of community involvement in the form of reduced absenteeism, improved student behavior in school, and the pupils' attitudes and adjustment. Research from Spain demonstrates that community involvement also helped combat gender violence inside and outside of schools through the participation of different groups of women in the school (Oliver et al. 2009). It has also been argued that sustainable school and curricular reform requires community involvement (Arriaza 2004), as family literacy programs help parents to help their own children and allow their voices to be heard when decisions are made that affect their children's learning and development (Tett 2001).

Community involvement has the potential to develop inclusionary actions that are democratic in nature, fostering the democratic inclusion of parents and other community members and making them active key players in their education and partners in the education process. According to Freire (1993), this should not be pseudo-participation, but committed involvement. However, the optimal approach to understanding the contributions that community involvement makes for children's school success is to analyze actual examples. Rosenfeld and Tardieu (2000) report on the successful experience of families living in extreme poverty in a *banlieue* in Lille (France). Families became the allies of teachers and other administrators and created a "street library" to promote children's literacy. They also strove to develop the *Regional Education Project*, a study conducted by all inhabitants of the neighborhood to make the families of all children, particularly those from poorer demographics, partners in the school. A library was created to allow children to discover that they could enjoy learning, reading, writing and using computers and so that they could discover their own capacities and knowledge.

Apple and Beane (2007) describe the Fratney School, in Milwaukee (United States), which is located in a highly diverse neighborhood. Teachers and parents jointly ran the school. They developed a multicultural curriculum to address problems of discipline and disrespect for human differences among the students. Parents tend to participate more when they can have a meaningful influence in the decisions regarding the future of the school and their children's lives (Apple and Beane 2007). By participating in this school, neighbors and other community members were able to transform not only the school's programs and curriculum but also their neighborhood as a whole.

Fischman and Gandin (2007) report on a Brazilian experience, the *Escola Cidadâ*, which employed "participatory budgeting", a social form of community government. All of inhabitants of Porto Alegre had the opportunity to directly participate in municipal decisions. *Escola Cidadâ* was based on three main premises:

(a) schooling matters if it provides real opportunities for community members to be literate (in Freire's terms); (b) learning is only possible when teachers are aware of the link between the educative and the political domains of education; and (c) success depends on the school's capacity to involve the whole community in a shared project. The experience of *Escola Cidadâ* demonstrated advancements in terms of educational inclusion. Increased enrollment, reduced early school leaving and school failure, and decreased illiteracy in the city have been related to the cooperation, solidarity, participation, and democracy inherent to the pedagogical practices of this experience.

These examples of community involvement went beyond empowering individuals by providing them with greater freedom and control over their lives. They also empowered and enabled groups of individuals to take collective action and change the culture of entire communities.

6.2 Building Learning Communities Based on Successful Educational Actions

The INCLUD-ED project has collected evidence of success for each SEA identified. Additionally, the combined implementation of diverse SEAs has also been studied. Two of the longitudinal case studies conducted in Project 6 concerned two *schools as learning communities* in Spain. *Schools as learning communities* is a project that consists in the transformation of schools and their environment with the aim of achieving academic and social success for all students (Gatt et al. 2011). To pursue this aim, schools are implementing all of the SEAs simultaneously. Schools that have been transformed into *learning communities* are improving their academic achievement, reducing school dropout and promoting social cohesion. These communities (teachers, families, students, and community members) have committed to collaborate and exclusively implement evidence-based actions in their schools, meaning that they decided to transform their traditional settings and organizations into forms that research demonstrated are successful using existing resources and capitalizing upon the community's strengths. Over 120 schools, public and private, located in wealthy and low-income areas and with different levels of diversity, in different countries are implementing the Successful Educational Actions identified by the INCLUD-ED project.

The first *learning community* was born in 1978, created by Professor Ramon Flecha (Giner 2011). It was La Verneda Sant Martí, in Barcelona, Spain, an adult educational center (Sánchez 1999). Neighbors in that area began to meet on the streets to demand public services (such a public library, a school for adult learners, a place for elders, etc.). They occupied a building, held by the former government, now to provide free services to the community. Based on egalitarian dialogue and democratic participation, this school has been in place for three decades and provides community members with formal and informal education and the opportunity to read classic works of world literature in literary circles. The success of this school, from its inception, has led to international recognition in the scientific and educational communities (Sánchez 1999; Flecha 2000; Apple 2012).

For several years, the Centre of Research in Theories and Practices that Overcome Inequalities (CREA), at the University of Barcelona, has investigated how to further develop this successful educational perspective for implementation at the compulsory levels of education (from early childhood, primary to secondary education). This is how CREA developed the model of *learning communities* and, as a public research center, offered it to whoever wished to implement it. Initially, beginning in 1995, CREA members were responsible for bringing the scientific advice to the primary and secondary education centers to transform them into *learning communities*. From the beginning, this advice has met all of the international scientific community's requirements for both scientific rigor and ethics (democratic, non-sexist and non-racist), as well as those regarding plurality and an openness to all disciplines, democratic ideologies, methodologies, cultures, gender options, ages, forms of life, etc. This approach differs from those of many other research groups in our context that remain isolated within one discipline, culture or ideology. Eventually, various individuals and teams from other universities were included to collaborate on the task of advising schools interested in implementing the model. All members of the network of advisors for *schools as learning communities* have examined the scientific basis of this approach, both theoretical and practical. These individuals include doctors from universities such as Harvard (first in world rankings) and the University of Wisconsin-Madison, which is first-ranked in the specialties of Educational Psychology and Curriculum and Instruction.

The *learning communities* project is based on dialogic learning (Flecha 2000), a theory of learning which starts from the premise that learning primarily depends on the interactions and dialogues that the students have, not only with the teachers but also with the other students, their families and other members of the community. Dialogic learning collects the primary contributions of the Social Sciences, such as the theory of dialogic action (Freire 1970) and the theory of the communicative action (Habermas 1984), as well as the contributions of the socio-cultural theories of learning (Vygotsky 1978).

The process of transforming a school into a *learning community* entails the following phases:

1. *Sensitization.* This first phase consists of researchers explaining the scientific bases of the *learning communities* project, detailing the contributions of scientific research regarding actions of excellence that have demonstrated their potential for promoting school success and the improvement of coexistence for all children in plural and diverse contexts. The evidence is jointly analyzed by all participants—researchers, professionals, family members and other members of the community—in connection with a reflection on and analysis of new challenges in society and those faced by the particular school. This phase involves 30 h of training and relies on the participation of all teaching staff and most of the members of the educational community.

2. *Decision-making*. After the sensitization, the educational community decides to initiate the project with the commitment of all involved members or that of the majority of the teaching staff and the community as a whole. The decision entails a debate involving all persons in the educational community concerning what the transformation of their school into a *learning community* implies. Participating in a decision-making process is an element of training in democratic education for the students, teachers, families and the rest of the agents in the educational community; it means that the stakeholders begin to experience the school as their own because it is the result of joint decisions and actions.

3. *Dreaming*. once the educational community has made the decision to transform their school into a *learning community*, all social agents—families, teachers, non-teaching staff, associations, entities, and the children—outline their dreams for their ideal school using the motto "the learning that we want for our children is the one we must also want for all boys and girls". All community members imagine and agree on the model of school they wish to use based on the principles of *learning communities*. This process takes place separately for each group (students, teachers, and families), and all of the dreams are collected and treated equally. Each school selects a means of representing the dreams of the entire educational community. Some schools depict the community's dreams using a dream train, some use clouds, others depict them on a large tree where every leaf is a dream, in a dream garden, and in many other diverse ways. The dreams are part of a new process of participation in the school and are clearly related to sharing opinions and decisions regarding the new school. This participatory process means that the entire community shares a dream for the school and generally represents the first time that the community is asked about what school they want for their children.

4. *Selecting priorities*. In this phase, the community revises the dreams and prioritizes them. To do so, the community begins by analyzing the knowledge, conditions and the resources available at that moment. To select the priorities, information is first collected on the history of the education center, the external image that it has, the means and the infrastructure on which it relies, the training of the teaching staff, the center's relationship with the environment, the potential of the administrative staff, the levels of student attendance and absenteeism, the students' academic results, family backgrounds with respect to culture, language, origins, etc. All of this information is used from positive perspective, never as a barrier. In combination with the dreams, this information is shared and debated among the entire community and then presented in a basic document stipulating all of the aspects to be improved, transformed and eliminated. Priorities are selected on the basis of the discussion of this information, first in the short term, and also indicating the actions to be implemented in the medium and long run.

5. *Planning*. Once the priorities have been selected, an assembly is held that the entire educational community participates in and decisions are made regarding planning and the different *mixed committees* to be created. These committees will be responsible for pursuing the various priorities. During this process, it is

important to define the functions of each committee while considering that: they are all equally valid; they need to be heterogeneous (formed by teaching staff, families, other professionals and community members, and students on some occasions); everyone can participate; and they have autonomy and decision-making capacity that needs to be confirmed by the School Council. Examples of types of mixed committees are the learning committee, the volunteers committee, the infrastructure committee, the coexistence committee, etc. A *management committee* coordinates and monitors the progress of all the other mixed committees. The management committee comprises representatives from each mixed committee and the school principal.

Empirical data demonstrate the progress in academic achievement and other improvements accomplished by *schools as learning communities* since the implementation of the SEAs. This is the case for the two *learning communities* that were followed in the longitudinal case studies assessed by the INCLUD-ED project. Both schools are located in highly socio-economically deprived areas, and both of them reduced early school leaving and increased academic achievement. For instance, in one of the school cases investigated for INCLUD-ED, absenteeism for the 2006–2007 school year was 30 %, in 2007–2008 it was reduced to 10 % and has been sporadic since then. Student enrolment has been increasing since the school was transformed into a *learning community*. In 2010, the percentage of students grew by 27.66 % relative to the previous year, and in 2011 the increase was 10.56 %.

On the basis of empirical evidence, the European Commission and the European Council have recommended the use of *learning communities* to address early school leaving in Europe. *Schools as learning communities* have become a common effort that involve teachers, pupils, families and stakeholders to implement the Successful Educational Actions that improve school performance and social cohesion for all children.

The positive impact of *schools as learning communities* in diverse social dimensions and policy areas has been recognized in three Council recommendations, conclusions, and communications in the category of current educational needs: promote inclusive practices and reduce early school leaving. These documents are as follows:

- *Council conclusions of* 11 *May* 2010 *on the social dimension of education and training* (2010/C 135/02). In these conclusions, with respect to early and school education, the Council invites the member states to: "Promote successful inclusive education approaches for all pupils, including those with special needs, by making schools *learning communities* in which a sense of inclusion and mutual support is nurtured and in which the talents of all pupils are recognized".
- *Communication from the EC* (*January* 2011). *Tackling early school leaving: A key contribution to the Europe* 2020 *Agenda*. This document states: "Schools as 'learning communities' agree on a common vision, basic values and objectives of school development. It increases the commitment of pupils,

teachers, parents and other stakeholders and supports school quality and development. 'Learning communities' inspire both teachers and pupils to seek improvement and take ownership of their learning processes. It also creates favourable conditions for reducing school dropout and for helping pupils at risk of dropping out".

- *Council Recommendation on policies to reduce early school leaving (June 2011) (10544/11).* This recommendation states that interventions implemented at the level of the school or training institution to reduce early school leaving could include: "Developing schools into learning communities based on a common vision for school development shared by all stakeholders, using the experience and knowledge of all, and providing an open-minded, inspiring and comfortable environment to encourage young people to continue education and training".

As a result of the publication and dissemination of the INCLUD-ED project's results, a growing number of public authorities and regional governments in Spain are adopting the *learning communities* project as a model to promote in their regions. For instance, the regional ministry of Education of the Andalusian Government passed a regulation on 8 June 2012 that establishes the process of registering and renewing a school as a *learning community* and creates the Andalusian Network of Learning Communities. This regulation seeks to establish the process by which schools receiving public funds from the Andalusian Government will be able to request recognition as *learning communities* or the ability to continue to pursue the project. It has created the Andalusian Network of Learning Communities, which is made up of schools that are recognized as adopters of the project.

The governments of an increasing number of Spanish municipalities are also expressing interest in *schools as learning communities*. In this regard, an agreement for extending SEAs to the schools and communities in the city of Rivas-Vaciamadrid, in Madrid, Spain, for the period 2010–2015 was signed by the city council of Rivas-Vaciamadrid and the University of Barcelona. This agreement implied the following main activities: trainings and assessments in schools that wish to implement the SEAs identified by INCLUD-ED and the training and assessment of professionals from different areas on the implementation of successful actions identified by INCLUD-ED. The SEAs have already been implemented in all primary schools in the municipality, meaning that approximately 200 schools are benefitting from the results of this research, and some of those schools have already begun their transformations into *learning communities*.

The results of INCLUD-ED are also having a relevant impact in the schools of other European countries. Through the Project *ChiPE: Children's personal epistemologies: Capitalising children's and families' knowledge in schools towards effective learning and teaching* (2013–2015) funded by the 7th Framework Programme of European research, Marie Curie actions, and conducted at the University of Cambridge, some of the results of the INCLUD-ED project are being further explored. This research includes the analysis of how schools working as *learning communities* prevent early school leaving and create an inclusive ethos. More specifically, the ways in which schools working as *learning communities* impact on teachers, children and families' epistemological beliefs and the ways in which this connects to children's diverse out-of-school knowledge are being analysed. One of the preliminary results of this project is that three schools in the United Kingdom have started to implement different SEAs and to become interested in the process of transformation into *learning communities*. Importantly, in the framework of this project a relationship has been established with the HertsCam Network co-ordinated by David Frost at the University of Cambridge Faculty of Education. This network is founded on principles that resonate with those of INCLUD-ED in that it empowers teachers and other community members to take the initiative and exercise leadership in collaborative relationships. The principles of leadership for learning, particularly in relation to shared leadership are operationalized in ways which enable practitioners to engage in scholarship and activism in both national and international contexts.

However the impact of INCLUD-ED's results and the proliferation of *schools as learning communities* have not only been observed in Europe but also on the other side of the Atlantic, particularly through the work of the Instituto Natura[1] in Brazil and other Latin American countries. The Instituto Natura was created in 2010, which represents the institutionalization of the social programs that Natura, a Brazilian company, has been developing since 1990. The transparent and innovative ethical stance of the company has been consistently recognized with several prizes and awards. It has been ranked first on lists of the most sustainable companies and the best corporate citizens. The Natura Institute was founded with the intention of developing a quality education that opens up horizons, widens consciences and generates opportunities, to create the basis for a better world. Last year, together with other collaborators, the Institute boasted programs and projects affecting 27 State secretaries, 3,300 municipalities in the country, 72,000 schools, 140,000 teachers and 3 million students from across Brazil. Their vision and mission is: "to create the conditions for all citizens to form a *learning community*". With this aim, the Institute initiated research, forums and international meetings with the objective of making this vision a reality. This is how it contacted with CREA-UB (Centre of Research in Theories and Practices that Overcome Inequalities of the University of Barcelona) and its Brazilian counterpart in research on *learning communities*, the NIASE (Núcleo de Investigação e Ação Social e Educativa) located at the University of Sao Carlos. After several meetings between the representatives of Instituto Natura, CREA and NIASE, as well as visits by the Instituto Natura's representatives to different *learning communities* in Spain, the III International Meeting of Learning Communities was held in Sao Paulo (Brazil) in April 2013, which gathered more than 300 persons from the third sector, civil and social organizations of different types, *learning communities* that are currently operating in Brazil, universities, policy-makers at the local and national levels, and representatives of the "international operations" that Natura has in Mexico, Chile,

---

[1] http://www.institutonatura.org.br/.

Argentina, Peru and Colombia. This event included a presentation of the project that won numerous supporters, such as the Secretary of State in Sao Paulo, different institutions and a clear commitment from the Municipal Secretary of Rio de Janeiro to promote *learning communities* in the city's network of public schools. At present, three schools have already become *learning communities* in Brazil (Garcia-Ajofrin 2013; Instituto Natura 2013).

Furthermore, the first scientific trainings on *learning communities* have begun in Peru and Guatemala, in collaboration with universities, organizations and NGOs in those countries. Sensitizations phases in Mexico and Colombia have also been planned. The dream that began in the Adult School of La Verneda-St Martí is thus expanding worldwide based on the evidence of success in the lives of the many children, adults, teachers, families and communities involved in the project. Also, recently, the Organization for Economic Cooperation and Development (OECD 2012) indicated that *schools as learning communities* is a model of a successful innovative learning environment.

References

Apple, M. W. & Beane, J. A. (2007). *Democratic Schools. Lessons in Powerful Education.* Portsmouth, NH: Heinemann.

Apple, M. W. (2012). *Can Education Change Society?.* New York: Routledge.

Arriaza, G. (2004). *Making Changes that Stay Made: School Reform and Community Involvement.* Project Muse: University of North Carolina Press.

Buckingham, D. (2005). *Children in Communication about migration. Final Report.* 5th Framework Programme. Key Action: Improving the Socio-economic Knowledge Base. Citizen and Governance in a knowledge-based society. HPSE-CT-2001-00048. Directorate-General for Research. Brussels: European Commission.

Delgado-Gaitan, C. (2001). *The Power of Community. Mobilizing for Family and Schooling.* Lanham: Rowmand and Littlefield.

Epstein, J. L. (2001). *School, Family and Community Partnerships: Preparing Educators and Improving Schools.* Boulder: Westview Press.

Epstein, J. L. (2004). Foreword. In P. A. Edwards (Ed.), *Children's literacy development: Making it happen through school, family and community involvement* (pp. ixxiv). Boston: Pearson Education.

Epstein, J. L., & Sheldon, S. B. (2006). Moving forward: Ideas for research on school, family and community partnerships. In C. F. Conrad & R. Serlin (Eds.), *SAGE handbook for research in education: Engaging ideas and enriching inquiry* (pp. 117–137). Thousand Oaks, CA: Sage Publications.

Faires, J., Nichols, W. B., & Rickelmann, R. J. (2000). Effects of Parental Involvement in developing competent readers in First grade. *Reading Psychology, 21,* 195–215.

Fischman, G. E., & Gandin, L. A. (2007). Escola cidada and critical discourse of educational hope. In P. McLaren & J. Kincheloe (Eds.), *Critical pedagogy: where are we now?* (pp. 209–223). New York: Petere Lang.

Fitzgerald, J. (2001). Can minimally trained college student volunteers help young at-risk students to read better? *Reading Research Quarterly, 36,* 28–46.

Flecha, R. (2000). *Sharing words.* Lanham, M.D: Rowman & Littlefield.

Freire, P. (1993). *The pedagogy of the oppressed.* London: Penguin.

Freire, P. (1970). *Pedagogy of the oppressed.* London: Continuum International.

Frome, P. M., & Eccles, J. S. (1998). Parents' influence on children's achievementrelated perceptions. *Journal of Personality and Social Psychology, 74*(2), 435–452.

García, E. (2002). *Student cultural diversity. understanding and meeting the challenge.* Boston: Houghton Mifflin Company.

Garcia-Ajofrin, L. (2013). Las comunidades de Aprendizaje llegan a Brasil. *Periodico Escuela, 3.993*(1.263), 31.

Gatt, S., Ojala, M., & Soler, M. (2011). Promoting social inclusion counting with everyone: learning communities and INCLUD-ED. *International Studies in Sociology of Education, 21* (1), 33–47.

George, R., & Kaplan, D. (1998). A structural model of parent and teacher influences on science attitudes of eighth graders: Evidence from NELS: 88. *Science Education, 82*(1), 93–109.

Giner, E. (2011). *Amistad deseada. Aportaciones de Jesús Gómez y Ramón Flecha que están acercando la realidad a nuestros sueños.* Barcelona: Hipatia Editorial.

Grolnick, W. S., Kurowski, C. O., & Gurland, S. T. (1999). Family processes and the development of children's self-regulation. *Educational Psychologist, 34,* 3–14.

Habermas, J. (1984). *The theory of communicative action. Volume I: Reason and the rationalisation of society.* Boston, MA: Beacon.

Harvard Family Research Project. (2007). *Family Involvement makes a difference,* 2 (Winter).

Instituto Natura. (2013). Brasil impulsa las CdA. *Periodico Escula. Suplemento Comunidades de Aprendizaje. N.9, Transferibilidad de las Actuaciones Educativas de Éxito.*

Jordon, G. E., Snow, C. E., & Porche, M. V. (2000). Project EASR: The effect of a family literacy project on kindergarten students early literacy skills. *Reading Research Quarterly, 35,* 524–546.

Lave, J., & Wegner, E. (1991). *Situated learning: legitimate peripheral participation.* New York: Cambridge University Press.

OECD (2012). Innovative Learning Environments. Inventory Case Study. Directorate for Education. Centre for Educatinal Research and Innovation, OECD. Retrieved November 29, 2013 from http://www.oecd.org/edu/ceri/49930737.pdf.

Oliver, E., Soler, M., & Flecha, R. (2009). Opening schools to all (women): efforts to overcome gender violence in Spain. *British Journal of Sociology of Education, 30*(2), 207–218.

Paratore, J. R., H., A., Krol-Sinclair, B., Duran P. (1999). Discourse between teachers and latino parents during conferences based on home literacy portfolios. *Education and Urban Society, 32,* 58–82.

Ponzetti, J. J., & Dullin, W. (1997). Parent education in Washington State even family literacy programs. *Early Childhood Education Journal, 25*(1), 23–29.

Rosenfeld, J. M., & Tardieu, B. (2000). *Artisans of democracy: How ordinary people, families in extreme poverty, and social institutions become allies to overcome social exclusion.* Maryland: University Press of America.

Sánchez, M. (1999). La Verneda Sant Martí. A school where people dare to dream. *Harvard Educational Review, 69*(3), 320–335.

Sanders, M., & Sheldon, S. (2009). *Principal matter: A guide to school, family and community partnerships.* California: Corwin.

Schuler, D. (1996). *New community networked: Wired for Change.* New York: ACM Press.

Teddie, C., & Reynolds, D. (2000). *The international handbook of school effectiveness research.* London: Falmer Press.

Tett, L. (2001). Parents as problems or parents as people? Parental involvement programmes, schools and adult educators. *International Journal of Lifelong Education, 20*(3), 188–198.

Vygotsky, L. S. (1978). *Mind in society: Development of higher psychological processes.* Cambridge: Harvard University Press.

Watkins, K. (2007). *Classrooms as learning communities: What's in it for Schools.* Great Britain: Routledge.

Wells, G. (1999). *Dialogic inquiry: towards a sociocultural practice and theory of education.* New York: Cambridge University Press.

Chapter 7
Integrative Actions for Social Inclusion (Employment, Political Participation, Access to Housing and Health)

This chapter discusses the relationship between education and other areas of society, with a particular focus on social inclusion/exclusion in employment, health, housing and political participation. Beginning with the literature on these close relationships, particular educational actions that have demonstrated positive results will be described and discussed. Successful cooperative actions, for instance, have a proven ability to create sustainable employment and job security. Examples of health literacy and financial literacy have contributed to reduce health problems and improve access to housing. In this vein, this chapter will focus in a case study of a poor neighborhood where successful actions in a number of social areas have been implemented through a Dialogic Inclusion Contract that involved the participation of all residents in the decision-making process.

Many studies have demonstrated the connections between educational success and inclusion in other areas of society (Castells et al. 1999). For decades, data collected on the different dimensions of social exclusion have indicated the long-standing association between educational levels and being accepted and included in society (Brandsma 2002; European Commission 2004). Social groups that tend to receive less formal education are more often excluded from the main areas of society (Pilgram et al. 2001; Social Exclusion Unit 2001; European Commission 2002).

Moreover, extensive research has demonstrated that education is one of the most important strategies, if not the most important, for improving access to employment, health, housing and other forms of participation in the broader society (Mircea and Dorobantu 2008). Those findings have led to research on how to improve educational success to promote social inclusion in all of these areas. These are what we termed Successful Educational Actions (SEAs) in the preceding chapters.

The focus of this chapter is not the educational arena but rather the interventions developed in each area of society. In particular, INCLUD-ED researchers have identified the ways that education is integrated into effective mixed interventions designed to improve inclusion in housing, employment, health, and overall social participation. We also explore the extent to which these interventions include educational components based on SEAs that make them more effective.

© The Author(s) 2015
R. Flecha (Ed.), INCLUD-ED Consortium, *Successful Educational Actions for Inclusion and Social Cohesion in Europe*, SpringerBriefs in Education,
DOI 10.1007/978-3-319-11176-6_7

In the next sections, we briefly describe INCLUD-ED's results on this topic. First, we compile a literature review on the role that education plays in interventions implemented in the four areas of society and contrast these findings with the experiences of professionals and community members in the fields explored. Second, we briefly summarize the main findings of our cross-case analysis of 18 Integrative Actions (IA). Third, we present the concept and examples of Integrative Successful Actions (ISA) and the Dialogic Inclusion Contract (DIC) as an example of a process that has been shown to facilitate the effective implementation of the ISAs.

7.1 Education Within Actions for Social Inclusion

The research has demonstrated that most actions designed to address social exclusion in the areas of employment, health, housing and political participation included educational provisions. Furthermore, INCLUD-ED studied how inclusion in these areas can be improved from the perspective of education when the latter is based on the SEAs. To summarize the findings and highlight those that are the most innovative, we present three key ideas here.

7.1.1 Increasing Employment Possibilities: Inclusive Vocational Training

The project identified the need to develop vocational training that promotes both sustainable and effective entry into the labor market and options to return to the educational system as a crucial element for avoiding long-term unemployment. Traditional vocational training, designed to immediately place students in the labor market (Kettunen 1997; Wolbers 2000; Cruikshank 2007), has not always considered the possibility that the individuals involved would return to the academic track. Researchers have found that this option should be maintained to reduce youth unemployment, especially among those who are more vulnerable to social exclusion.

The INCLUD-ED project highlighted vocational training programs that allow students to return to the educational system to gain certifications such as the baccalaureate, therefore compensating for the negative effects of early tracking. These programs have two main characteristics. First, instead of designing vocational training curriculums that exclusively focus on specific skills for concrete occupations, they include the academic subjects necessary for higher qualification, in conjunction with workplace-related skills. This structure guarantees that youths in these programs pursue a more thorough and integrated curriculum and therefore acquire both the key competences for lifelong learning that they will need in the labor market (Santa Cruz et al. 2011). In addition, they gain the ability to access academic tracks that can lead to higher education and better working conditions in the long term. Second, these vocational training programs incorporate academic ladders that allow students to advance into higher education. As a result, all of these measures can make the system more flexible and equitable, removing the barriers that previously kept socially excluded youth from returning to academic education.

An example of an inclusive vocational training program is that offered by the Mondragon Cooperative Corporation. The cooperative included a professional school from its inception; at present, education and training is one of its main principles. The Politeknika Ikastegia Txorierri is a secondary and vocational education cooperative training center that provides courses leading to a bachelor's degree, as well as vocational educational courses. It focuses on serving local industry, in close collaboration with local companies, and is simultaneously committed to the integral and lifelong learning of its students. A dual character defines this training center, as it facilitates access to both university studies and the labor market.

7.1.2 Inclusion in Political Participation: Involving End-Users in Decision-Making

Similar to what we defined above as community participation in decision-making in schools, an element that frequently arose in both the literature review and the interviews was the urgent need to open up decision-making processes in different social areas (European Commission 2006). Additionally, our findings support the need to ensure that this participation is oriented towards implementing successful actions in different areas of society.

> All of us on the board, all the volunteers, we all are in the assemblies. It is not the teachers who decide, we do. [This is important] because we in the community know what we want, for instance, we know if we want to do dance or literature.
>
> School family member (Spain)

There is a substantial body of literature analyzing actions that have been shown to be successful in engaging end-users in decision-making and designing policies, that is, in promoting empowered participatory governance (Fung and Wright 2001). Some examples are participatory budgets or citizens' assemblies, which lead to tangible social improvements. The INCLUD-ED project has demonstrated that it is essential to create spaces for dialogue with the end-users while avoiding the presence of intermediaries. When citizens are eager to participate in the dialogue and express their priorities and engage in the decisions that affect them, their families and their community, the result of this participation is a more efficient allocation of resources, as well as further social inclusion.

> In England, representatives of neighborhood associations are included in the management bodies, the administrative boards of hospitals, as a first step… also former patients are included, in such a way that there is not only the erudite opinion of doctors and directors in the management of hospitals but also those of the people who have received the service. But it is just beginning in our country.
>
>   Director of a hospital (UK)

Similarly, in the field of health, there are actions that have been successful in promoting the participation of vulnerable groups in decision-making that have not traditionally done so. This inclusion has been shown to help improve health systems, making them more efficient, equitable, and democratic. One of the most successful is direct citizen participation in the design, organization, and evaluation of health services. The health service authorities interviewed recognized that it is essential to include end-users in the design of health programs (Ottawa Charter for Health Promotion 1986; Xu et al. 1997). Therefore, we highlight the increasing need for dialogue and consent between the experts and end-users of health services. The same is true in housing, employment, welfare services and other social initiatives.

7.1.3 Focused Literacy to Enhance Access to Housing and Health

> We were frequently thinking what we could do, but it all stops because we do not know how to get to [the end-users]. There is no sense in making a program without including them in it. Before we make any new programs, we should conduct a focus group and ask them what they really need. We go to the school, or to a work organization or to a pensioner's association and determine the opinion of people, but in that way, we cannot cover dropouts.
>
>   Health professional (Slovenia)

Health literacy (Rudd et al. 1999) is identified as a successful action that can assist individuals with little formal education in improving their position within the health system. Health literacy means the ability to obtain, process, and understand basic information on health and necessary health services to make the most appropriate decisions. Health literacy offers numerous benefits. Individuals with more information on healthcare structures are better able to use them, and better information also has a positive impact on the health of the population itself. This is particularly important for members of certain vulnerable groups, such as women.

> We not only test the materials, but we also investigate the needs perceived in the vulnerable groups in the population (...) therefore our samples are oriented towards vulnerable groups and groups with educational deficits.
>
> When a population with low socio-educational levels has a service that is adapted, "tailored", made to measure, based on their needs, their diversity, and they have health services that are motivating and personalized, they can manage to respond to not only all aspects of life or healthcare provision but also to many areas in a way which is practically equivalent to the normal population.
>
> Responsible for health services (Slovenia)

In this vein, Sen (1999) and Stein (1997) argue that female education and literacy are important predictors of their health. They also emphasize the role of health education, literacy campaigns, and other initiatives in non-formal education as successful actions to improve the health of women and their children and families. These findings indicate that it is not so much an individual's level of education that impacts the effective access and use of healthcare services, but rather participation in educational activities that seek to improve access to and use of healthcare services. Therefore, actions that incorporate health literacy are fundamental. However, they should always be conducted in ways that consider the needs and desires of end-users; the research reveals that health literacy programs that do not address the needs and interests of individuals fail to achieve their objectives (Flecha et al. 2011).

Financial literacy also plays a crucial role in increasing the financial skills that allow individuals, especially those with less formal education, to better understand and manage their domestic finances (Harvard Joint Center for Housing Studies 2012). It is defined as the set of abilities and knowledge that allows individuals to understand financial issues related to domestic economic management. Thus education is widely regarded as a key element for address inequalities in this area. Researchers have demonstrated that financial literacy makes a significant difference in an individual's ability to access housing benefits.

The academic literature contains substantial evidence that financially literate individuals make better decisions regarding their mortgages and are more able to avoid potential fraud in either public or private housing (OECD 2005). Conversely, a lack of financial knowledge related to housing has negative consequences for end-users, especially those with little formal education. Individuals from disadvantaged backgrounds are more likely to become victims of housing abuse and fraud. For example, they may make poor decisions because they lack information or encounter misinformation on issues such as interest rate changes.

7.2 Integrative Actions: Contributions from a Cross-Case Analysis

We analyzed 18 Integrative Actions (IA), that is, actions that target education and one or more of the areas of society addressed in this project (employment, health, housing and political participation). These Integrative Actions were selected because they were effective in promoting social cohesion in their particular field of action. The cross-case analysis conducted by the INCLUD-ED project revealed six common elements that contributed to overcoming exclusion and strengthening social cohesion, which are described in more detail below.

7.2.1 Effective Networking to Optimize Resources

> **MURA Program (Slovenia)**
>
> It aims to identify, develop, implement and strengthen best practices in the field of socioeconomic and environmental development to achieve improved health and quality of life for individuals in the Pomurje region.
>
>   Selected results: The population of Pomurje began to eat more vegetables, drink less alcohol and smoke less.

Various analysts have described the power of networking and advocacy (Geddes 2000; Zippel 2004; De Stefano 2010) an aspect that is also identified in the Non-Discrimination and Equal Opportunities for All Framework Strategy (European Commission 2005). Similarly, in many of the cases we analyzed, joint and coordinated efforts between all actors involved in the community—public administrations, NGOs, and the private sector—were essential. Effective networking has thus been found to be a key element to optimize the use of resources.

For example, in the Health Promoting Schools Network and the MURA program, which provide training for a healthier lifestyle and are both located in Slovenia, various agents collaborated on a coordinated effort. A healthier lifestyle was included as a cross-curricular topic in schools and the community. This approach is fostering health promotion in schools as a more integral aspect of both the education and health domains in the region.

7.2.2 Involving Those Traditionally More Excluded in Recreating Successful Actions

Integrated Plan for the Roma people of Catalonia (Spain)

This is a public policy designed to analyze the situation of the Roma people in Catalonia and propose a series of actions in different social areas to be developed to address the exclusion experienced by the Roma community.

Selected results: the educational success of Roma students and especially girls increased; community participation by Roma people increased, primarily through associations.

Through the cross-case analysis, we identified an effective place for involving end-users, especially members of vulnerable groups, in decision-making processes: during the "recreation of successful actions". The Integrative Actions we studied occur in the context of certain local associations, educational centers, vocational training centers, and other social entities in which vulnerable groups participate in the process of recreating several successful actions. During the "recreation process", end-users discuss successful actions that have already been explained by professionals or researchers; they share their views and make recommendations for how to implement these actions in their own context. Therefore, vulnerable groups become the main actors in the decision-making process; they play an essential role when deciding and agreeing on the solution for the problems that the entire community faces. Moreover, the recreation process follows a key principle: decisions are made through egalitarian dialogue regardless of the position that each person occupies within the community. Thus they are made, as Habermas (1984) would say, on the strength of individuals' arguments, not on the power or the social position of those providing the arguments.

The Urbanitas Plan of the City of Albacete (Spain)

This initiative implemented various successful actions in several social areas to assist a deprived neighborhood's efforts to eliminate ghettoization, based on the Dialogic Inclusion Contract.

Selected results: improved academic results for children; increased community participation; improvements in neighbors' lifestyles; reduced unemployment.

Making decisions following this approach had numerous positive effects in improving the living conditions of individuals residing in deprived areas and who are at risk of exclusion. For instance, this approach was used to implement and coordinate two community intervention plans in Spain: the Urbanitas Plan in Albacete, and the course on canteen aids for Roma women, which was part of the Integrated Plan for the Roma People of Catalonia.

The training course for school canteen monitors targets Roma women excluded from the labor market with limited or no educational qualifications. Roma women with low educational attainment suffer a threefold situation of inequality: being a woman, belonging to a cultural minority, and not having access to education. This course helps to overcome these three inequalities. They are implemented in the most excluded neighborhoods, where educational activities are limited or do not exist. This course consists of vocational training that provides Roma women with an educational certificate and practical work experience in schools and is run by a non-profit association, the Roma Association of Women Drom Kotar Mestipen (which in the Roma language means Path to Freedom). The creation of spaces for dialogue has been essential to contribute to the labor market participation of these Roma women. These spaces were created in an attempt to give voice to those who are typically excluded from the decisions that concern them. In this case, the Roma women have been able to select the training that they need to find a job. The course was created at the request of these Roma women themselves. Having identified a lack of positive Roma role models for children in schools, these women dreamt, in the context of a dialogue in the Drom Kotar Mestipen Assembly, of being more present in schools to promote Roma role models among Roma pupils (Representative of Drom Kotar Mestipen, personal communication, February 22nd, 2011). They also participated in the planning and implementation of the activity: the course is organized by Roma women from the same neighborhood and is held there. This involved these women searching for appropriate facilities and engaging the course participants in promoting and disseminating the course to encourage greater involvement by Roma women in the area. The tailoring of the activities to the prior experience, skills, and needs of these women also stems from the inclusion of Roma voices and is regarded as a key element for the success of this Integrative Action. This means, for instance, adjusting the class hours to the requirements of Roma women and providing childcare during these trainings.

It is important to highlight that as a result of the training course for school canteen monitors, the participants obtained an educational qualification accredited by the Government of Catalonia and practical work experience in this area, which provides them with improved employment prospects. The program's success is due to both high rates of employment among the Roma women after the course and the positive influence that the presence of these women has had in the schools. These results contribute to improving social coexistence in schools. Roma women become role models, not only for Roma children but also for everyone.

Another action that is being developed in the context of the Integrated Plan for the Roma People of Catalonia are Roma student meetings organized by the Roma Association of Women Drom Kotar Mestipen. The goal is to increase the presence of Roma girls and women in training activities to both encourage young girls to remain in school through high school and university and promote training for adult Roma women. As a result of these meetings, which have been held twice annually since 1999, a network of solidarity has been created among Roma women, promoting an environment in which increasing numbers of girls are studying to graduate from university and more adult women are participating in training courses.

One of the actions included in both plans is the creation of spaces for dialogue and decision-making among individuals who have traditionally been excluded from such spaces. Projects that give voice to these groups are developing these types of spaces and creating networks through which more vulnerable individuals are participating.

Among the Integrative Actions encouraging members of vulnerable groups to participate both socially and politically, some facilitate direct conversations with government bodies at the local, regional, national, and European levels. Representatives of particularly vulnerable groups discuss and reflect on issues related to their social inclusion in areas such as employment, health, education, and housing, and policy-makers record their comments. This process is also used in the mixed committees developed in the context of the Dialogic Inclusion Contract, which became a successful tool for coordinating the transformation of the *La Milagrosa* neighborhood in Spain, as will be explained in the section titled " Integrative Successful Actions (ISA): the Dialogic Inclusion Contract".

> **FORUM's Resident Housing Workshops (Netherlands)**
>
> This is a local project with a training component designed to facilitate and promote the involvement of all residents in housing and residential development activities.
>
> Selected results: many residents of multicultural neighborhoods that were unaware of how the renovation plans worked learned about them and were able to have their houses renovated or renewed. As a result, many families' living conditions improved.

Another program that is increasing participation is the FORUM's Resident Housing Workshops (RHW) in the Netherlands. The RHW seeks to facilitate and promote the involvement of all residents in housing and residential development activities. In these multicultural spaces, neighbors have the opportunity to engage in dialogues and decision-making processes on topics of interest to them. These are spaces for dialogues between end-users and construction professionals in which residents directly participate in decisions concerning strategies to improve and restructure deprived urban areas. As they become more involved in community issues, residents can work to improve their living conditions.

Participants in the RHW are selected from multicultural neighborhoods that are about to be restructured and/or renewed. This project was designed based on the assumption that specific groups such as youths, the elderly, and the non-native population are poorly involved in processes of this type and very little knowledge has been accrued regarding the specific residential wishes and needs of these groups

(FORUM 2005, p. 15). Through the RHW, FORUM intends to address this by promoting a multicultural residential renewal process, encouraging the participation of all in the development of their communities and neighborhoods. In the long run, the aim of this intervention is to encourage the involvement of all the residents in future development plans proposed by the authorities and housing companies (FORUM 2005, p. 30).

The workshops follow five stages[1]: in the first phase (stage zero), all local parties involved, including the inhabitants, come together to discuss the RHW program and explain the tasks and role expected from each. The residents then interact with each other (stage 1) and discuss their respective backgrounds, lifestyles, housing and neighborhoods. Residents agree on several aspects concerning the remaining sessions, notably the applicable methodology and timeframe. The second stage consists of a discussion on the positive and negative aspects of the neighborhood. An exercise is also conducted that allows participants to state their housing preferences. Specific tasks such as taking pictures and analyzing their districts are assigned to each participant. Residents who are not directly affected by the regeneration of a specific area are invited to provide their contributions. Positive and negative experiences are discussed, and potential improvements to the neighborhood are identified. During the third stage, municipal authorities and housing companies explain what the urban renewal program consists of and what the development plans are. During this process, participants are encouraged to raise questions, seek explanations and voice their concerns and preferences. The participants are then shown how to create a blueprint of the renovation plans based on their experiences and knowledge. Finally, an architect supports the participants' efforts to translate their thoughts into projects. Participants then practice presenting the blueprints. They will then present these to an alderman, a housing company and resident organizations. This presentation, which occurs during the fourth stage, allows the residents' to directly express and present their most pressing residential needs to the main stakeholders (the municipality and housing company) (FORUM 2005, pp. 34–39). After the presentation, the proposed design is integrated into the regular plan developed by the housing companies and municipal authorities.

By stimulating and facilitating the participation of migrants and ethnic minorities in the development and improvement of residential spaces, the RHW are designed to promote their involvement in the processes of renewing their neighborhoods. The educational dimension inherent to this Integrative Action consists of a pedagogical process that leads to the formulation of the residents' wishes concerning residential renovations and guiding participants in participating in decision making processes. Participants, who tend not to be familiar with the overall decision-making process leading to the renovation of a neighborhood, are given the opportunity to participate and influence the process.

---

[1] FORUM official website, available at http://archief.forum.nl/woonateliers/index-engels.html Accessed 20 November 2013.

Overall, the direct participation of stakeholders and end-users is increasingly included in the definition of European policies, which emphasize more open methods of policy making that incorporate a wider range of actors in decision-making processes to promote citizenship and social cohesion. The research literature highlights the relevance of including the voices and demands of the various social actors who will be affected by a given policy (Puigvert et al. 2012). In addition, our analysis of the various Integrative Actions demonstrates that these actors will be more effective in solving problems when community integration programs are designed to include both the direct participation of social agents and evidence from empirical research. Overall, this combination helps to increase social cohesion.

7.2.3 Easy Access to Return to School

The INCLUD-ED project's analyses of some of the case studies reveals that when programs combine advising and career guidance with educational and training activities, they encourage students to return to school. This was the experience of three IAs in the UK and Austria. The *Young People at Risk of Offending Programme* in the UK supports entry into the labor market. The projects for women and young immigrants in the *Territorial Employment Pacts* (TEP) in Austria include in-school training for mothers; in addition, in its intensive vocational training, The *Stepping Stones Association* offers training and consulting on other social issues that affect employment decisions for girls in Austria.

Within the framework of the TEP in Austria, a project in Vienna's primary schools is organizing trainings in science, German language, math, art, culture, computers and technology for immigrant mothers lacking basic education. These women's participation in the training allowed them to learn the language and improve their basic education, and this is promoting these women's involvement in their children's learning in school, thereby improving the children's school careers. It also allows the women to enter gainful employment or start their own businesses. In addition, many of them participate in other training activities promoted by the Public Employment Agency, as they accomplish basic requirements such as language and basic education. Without the training received in these schools, these immigrant mothers would encounter numerous difficulties in finding employment and participating in vocational training, which requires a minimum set of basic skills (Territoriale Beschäftigungspakte in Österreich Zwischenbilanz 2011).

Thus, integrated educational programs combine three goals. They are designed to help members of the target groups enter the workforce. They also seek to guarantee that trainees can return to formal education or continue their training, and they provide training in other areas that may influence the new employees' professional decisions.

7.2.4 Individual Monitoring and Recognizing Previous Learning Experiences

DYNAMO (Austria)

An association of organizations that offers technical and educational support for vocational school students through individual learning coaching in small groups. Its main target group is young migrants and refugees aged 15–25.

The members of the association, such as DYNAMO, demand greater rights for these vulnerable groups and their education and labor inclusion.

Across the cases, we found that individualized plans are often identified as an effective strategy. They can exploit of previous, and not necessarily academic, learning. Moreover, individually tailored plans can better respond to specific needs. This approach is observed in a variety of Integrative Actions. For instance, successful programs provide advice for companies that hire young apprentices who are members of vulnerable groups. Alternatively, similar to the Stepping Stones Association for Girls in Austria, they offer monitoring and individual counseling for new employees. This counseling, whether provided to the companies or to the young women, has improved women's access to jobs that were traditionally considered masculine. This is particularly important because most of these women are of immigrant origin; thus, this initiative has provided them with new and improved work opportunities.

Certain provisions are necessary to guarantee that vocational training measures are effective. Some successful training programs begin by evaluating and acknowledging the skills and competences that the applicants already possess, such as multilingualism, or skills arising from their experience in the informal economy; one example is the Dynamo Network in Austria. The Into Work Development in the UK provides spaces for dialogue for persons with disabilities, enabling them to share their experiences and jointly seek strategies to overcome barriers to labor market access.

7.2.5 Increased Participation Through Close Referents

Another common element found across these Integrative Actions is the extension of participation in educational and training programs when individuals from a single community or social group are involved. This is particularly important among vulnerable groups.

One example is the *Red Connecta* in Spain, which is responsible for the public provision of computer access in low-SES neighborhoods designed to address the digital divide affecting youths aged 13–30 in these contexts. Members of vulnerable groups directly participated in the design and implementation of the program, which can constantly adjust its activities based on the needs that arise as these members discuss their experiences. Participation rates in the program are rising because a high percentage of the students ultimately work or volunteer for the program or other community projects, while some continue with further training. The involvement of former students as volunteers or coordinators serves as a positive reference for other youth who then also decide to participate.

7.2.6   Actions Based on Solidarity

Fondazione Casa Amica (Italy)

The aim of this volunteer non-profit is to facilitate access to housing for migrants and Italians living in poor conditions or facing exclusion. One of their projects is "Casa a colori", which focuses on protecting children and supporting single mothers.

Training in different fields is a key element of all actions that promote access to housing for members of vulnerable groups. Here, the relevant educational provisions range from financial literacy and negotiated agreements with local banks, to educational activities that promote empowerment, such as those of the *Casa a Colori* program, managed by *Fondazione Casa Amica* in Italy. Families participate in various educational activities that also improve their life conditions in other social areas.

This organization provides housing training and support for various vulnerable groups. For instance, regarding migrants, the association manages temporary housing for the accommodation of medium-term immigrant groups. Its activities include training in the proper use and maintenance of accommodations and facilities, rules of communal living and self-management. Furthermore, the association builds and manages housing for single mothers with children facing poor housing conditions and at risk social situations. It plans and implements, in conjunction with the local authority, residential placement locations in housing developments for disadvantaged individuals. The primary objective is to promote paths to individual independence.

Cooperativa Sociale Biloba (Italy)

This is a pilot project that establishes strategies for the integrated planning of urban ecosystems, the development of community and active citizenship, the prevention of discomfort, and to promote well-being.

Shared living situations are identified as an effective alternative that promotes participation in community actions. This idea is the basis for *Cooperativa Sociale Biloba*.

The cooperative establishes strategies for the integrated planning of urban ecosystems, the development of community and active citizenship, the prevention of discomfort and the promotion of well-being. The pilot project *"Coabitazione solidale"*, sponsored by the Municipality of Turin and coordinated by the Cooperative, has the primary objective of promoting the development of community and social networks in the district and developing cohabitation agreements among young volunteers (18–30 years old) while maintaining the value of solidarity. The project encourages youths to participate in the community and facilitates their access to housing. Youths receive low-rent apartments in neighborhoods where many face social exclusion. In exchange, they sign an agreement to provide 10 h of volunteer work in the neighborhood's social and educational projects, which promote community participation and improve social relationships.

Integrative Actions related to housing share two main elements. First, they are based on fostering solidarity among individuals, many of whom are living in disadvantaged situations. Second, they aim to empower participants by ensuring that they have all of the information they need when they make any decision regarding housing and understand various ways of accessing housing and improving their living conditions.

7.3 Integrative Successful Actions: The Dialogic Inclusion Contract

Based on the knowledge of the positive effect that Integrative Actions have on social inclusion, INCLUD-ED was interested in researching those Integrative Actions connected to the Successful Educational Actions (SEAs) previously studied. We define these as Integrative Successful Actions (ISAs), which target one or more areas of society (employment, health, housing, and social and political participation) related to the SEAs. In addition, the ISAs have demonstrated progress in expanding the access of the most vulnerable groups.

One of the Integrative Actions analyzed was the URBANITAS Plan in the *La Estrella* and *La Milagrosa* neighborhoods (Albacete, Spain). This case study provided relevant insights into improvements in the different areas of society and led to increasing social cohesion. In addition, the procedure used to implement the plan in this context, the Dialogic Inclusion Contract, demonstrated its ability to ensure the development of Integrative Actions that succeed in promoting social cohesion and the social and educational inclusion of vulnerable groups.

Successful Educational Actions were the basis for developing the URBANITAS Plan. It began with the transformation of one school in a poor ghetto neighborhood we studied in Project 6. The school implemented *interactive groups*, *dialogic reading*, afterschool library tutoring, and various successful types of family and community participation, which led to numerous successes. First, the children's average grades doubled in six competence areas only one year after these SEAs were implemented, and they continued to improve over the next few years. In addition, through various processes, the residents became more fully included in the neighborhood in terms of employment, health access, housing, and social and political participation. For instance, when family members were involved in family education programs or participated in the decision-making processes at the school, their children's achievement improved, but there was also a process of empowerment that increased their confidence, involvement in the community and, finally, their employment opportunities. The transformation of the school was linked to the development of ISAs. Two examples are the worker's cooperative promoted by the Association Miguel Fenollera and the Weekend Center. Both examples integrate actions in education, employment and social participation. The development of these ISAs was possible after a dialogic process of community participation in decision-making, the Dialogic Inclusion Contract, which is described below.

7.3.1 The Dialogic Inclusion Contract: A Dialogic Procedure to Overcome Social Exclusion

The Dialogic Inclusion Contract (DIC) is a dialogic procedure in which researchers, end-users, and policymakers recreate successful actions through egalitarian dialogue. Researchers provide information on actions that have proven successful elsewhere, according to the international scientific community. Next, these actions are recreated in the new context through dialogue with the residents and policy-makers (Aubert 2011). These agreements are reached through a discussion process, in which all the views of the different stakeholders are evaluated on the strengths of their arguments. That is, they are valued according to the contribution they make toward achieve the ultimate goal of the plan: to improve the living conditions of marginalized communities and help individuals to escape the ghetto (Padrós et al. 2011). Through this process, specific actions are selected that will transform the different social areas. These actions are based on other actions previously identified as successful, both in education and various fields of social policy. The aim of this process is to ensure that the Integrative Successful Actions resulting from the process fulfill the first and second criteria. When researchers, end-users, and policy-makers engage in an egalitarian and collaborative dialogue in which they compare empirical evidence with the end-users' knowledge, they make it much more likely that the resulting decisions regarding the implementation of the Integrative Actions will respond to the end-users' needs.

The DIC was implemented in the neighborhoods of *La Estrella* and *La Milagrosa*, two of the most underprivileged neighborhoods in Spain, located in the outskirts of the City of Albacete. Citizens in this area suffer from high levels of poverty because their primary source of income is temporary and informal jobs such as selling scrap metal; over 35 % of the working age population depend on social welfare. These individuals are primarily Roma and immigrants, 7 % are illiterate and 79 % have not completed basic education (Ministerio de Educación, Políticas Sociales y Deporte 2008). Through the DIC, residents of the two neighborhoods and the city decided to implement ISAs with the objective of integrating these individuals into society and addressing their high levels of poverty, precarious labor conditions, and low levels of education. Instead of the former situation in which the administration and local associations made such decisions, there were several assembly gatherings for different associations, churches, teachers, families from the school, neighbors, local officials and researchers. The researchers provided information on successful actions in various areas of society, and through dialogue, these actions were recreated for the local context. In this way, the DIC leads to the recreation of SEAs and ISAs in an inclusive and egalitarian process and, therefore, guarantees the implementation of actions for success.

7.3.2 Integrative Successful Action: Worker-Owned Cooperative—From Successful Schools to Successful Worker Cooperatives

One of the main challenges that the neighborhood faced was the lack of employment opportunities. Through the DIC, a dialogue between researchers, policymakers and community members (end-users) was launched with a presentation on creating employment in similar contexts. One of the successful actions presented was the Mondragon Cooperative Group. Created in the mid-1950s, it has managed to transform a deeply deprived valley into one that has the lowest level of income inequality in Europe, while achieving the lowest unemployment rate in Spain and being the country's seventh largest industrial group. Mondragon's educational base is strongly connected to the open intellectual debate that has characterized it from the beginning. Mondragon develops its own intellectual foundation based on influences from numerous perspectives and consistently employs them to help transform its economy, society and culture. The educational network of Mondragon is rooted in all of the group's previous experiences. It comprises several vocational training centers and one university: the Mondragon Unibertsitatea. One of its key characteristics is its close and permanent relationship with the labor market, which allows it to tailor its programs to meet the real needs of Montragon Corporation's companies and organizations (Flecha 2012).

A discussion was initiated regarding activities in the informal economy, in which many families were already working as street vendors, construction workers, cleaners, caretakers for the elderly, etc. Some community members envisioned becoming social workers. The discussion turned to how the informal economy could be organized more efficiently and could provide alternative forms of self-employment in a cooperative framework. The main idea was to draw on the strengths of the community, identifying possible sources of employment and facilitating the conditions for better jobs.

After several community assemblies, the decision was made to develop an action plan to create a cooperative. The Miguel Fenollera NGO, already working in the community, supported the process of identifying market needs and jobs in the neighborhood and beyond. Families involved in the association participated in this process; some had extensive knowledge of business, the economy, and the labor market. The NGO relied on the support and counsel of a training team at the University of Castilla-La Mancha to create the cooperative; one of the team's priorities is to train and prepare members of the cooperative in business areas that are being developed, building on their existing background knowledge. The knowledge, experience, and resources of this and other entities were placed at the service of the community to create a cooperative that generates decent self-employment that is stable and sustainable, offering effective and useful services to the community and surrounding areas.

One year after Miguel Fenollera[2] was created, at the beginning of November 2011, under difficult economic conditions in Spain, the cooperative was creating employment for the families in the *La Estrella* and *La Milagrosa* neighborhoods. The eleven members of the cooperative, ten of whom live in these neighborhoods, have indefinite contracts. None of them had stable employment before the creation of the Cooperative, and they are an example of personal and family transformation. One section of the cooperative is the Attention Office for Field Workers, which has employed 317 people and concluded 570 contracts. During September, October and November, nearly 150 workers were permanently employed; 18 individuals in the *La Estrella* and *La Milagrosa* neighborhoods have internships related to diverse activities that take place in the neighborhoods; 124 individuals have participated in trainings since September 2010, some of them in coordination with social services and the employment service of the Albacete Council. The cooperative expects to continue creating additional positions in cleaning services, industry, refurbishing and home repairs, building, telemarketing, and as sport, free time and leisure instructors.

7.3.3 Integrative Successful Action: The Weekend Center—Learning for All in the Neighborhood

The leisure activities developed by this association with the aim of preventing delinquency and drug consumption have gone from working with 40 to working with 400 children aged 4–16, when integrated in the Centro FINDE.
Social educator

---

[2] Miguel Fenollera Cooperative official web site, available at http://www.coopmfenollera.com/ Accessed 20 November 2013.

The Weekend Center [*Centro FINDE*] was created as a response to the community's demand for a space where youth could spend their afterschool time in the evening and on the weekends. More than half of the neighborhood's residents are under 30. The Center applies the SEAs identified by the INCLUD-ED project, such as extending children's learning time through afterschool programs and clubs where neighbors collaborate to identify and develop educational and cultural components through dialogue.

The Weekend Center created an alternative for youth to being on the streets. Thus it addressed potential risks, such as the dealing and consumption of drugs, and enabled youths to participate in educational, cultural and leisure activities—resources they often do not find at home. Open from Friday at 5 p.m. until Sunday at 8:30 p.m., the primary school facilities are open to offer a wide variety of activities, around three main axes. The first axis, learning and training, includes activities that help foster learning among children and youths based on successful actions, such as a tutored library and additional educational support. The second axis concerns increasing the motivation of youths to learn and facilitating their access to and use of ICT. On this axis, there are plans to create a WiFi network for the two neighborhoods to provide residents with access to the Internet and its resources, and residents will be able to find jobs online and take workshops on producing online content. The third axis focuses on overcoming conflicts in the neighborhood caused by the consumption and trafficking of drugs. In response to demands by participants, a range of cultural and sports activities are being developed.

> Before the existence of Centro Finde, there was no public service available. Today, there are between 30 to 50 people taking part in cultural, educational and social activities, who formerly were on the streets and exposed to unhealthy habits such as drug addiction.
>
> Neighbor

The Weekend Center provides children and youth and other community members with an educational and social space that involves all neighborhood groups in transforming the educational and social context. This implies that individuals who have traditionally been excluded from such spaces are now participating in decision-making in ways that help overcome their situation of exclusion. With the Weekend Center, the children and youth are no longer left on the streets when the professionals finish their workweek and go home. The Weekend Center has deeply transformed the residents' sense of participation and improved educational results and the neighborhood's social life.

References

Aubert, A. (2011). Moving beyond social exclusion through dialogue. *International Studies in Sociology of Education, 21*(1), 63–75.

Brandsma, J. (2002). *Education, equality and social exclusion. Final synthesis report*. Brussels: DG Research

Castells, M., Freire, P., Flecha, R., Giroux, H., Macedo, D., & Willis, P. (1999). *Critical education in the new information age*. Lanham, MD: Roman & Littlefield.

Cruikshank, J. (2007). Lifelong learning and the new economy: rhetoric or reality? *Education Canada, 47*, 32–36.

De Stefano, L. (2010). Facing the water framework directive challenges: A baseline of stakeholder participation in the European Union. *Journal of Environmental Management, 91*(6), 1332–1340.

European Commission. (2002). Communication from the commission on 20 November 2002 on European benchmarks in education and training: follow-up to the Lisbon European Council (COM(2002) 629 Final). Retrieved November, 29, 2013, from http://europa.eu/legislation_summaries/education_training_youth/general_framework/c11064_en.htm

European Commission. (2004). *Early school leavers*. Brussels: Eurostat Metadata.

European Commission. (2005).Communication from the commission to the council, the European parliament, the European economic and social committee and the committee of the regions of 1 June 2005—non-discrimination and equal opportunities for all—a framework strategy [COM (2005)224—official journal C 236 of 24.9.2005]. Retrievied November, 29, 2013, from http://eur-lex.europa.eu/LexUriServ/LexUriServ.do?uri=COM:2005:0224:FIN:EN:PDF

European Commission. (2006). Accompanying document to the communication from the commission to the council and to the European parliament. *Efficiency and equity in European education and training systems*. Brussels: European Commission.

Flecha, A., García, R., & Rudd, R. E. (2011). Using health literacy in school to overcome inequalities. *European Journal of Education, 46*(2), 209–218.

Flecha, R. (2012). European research, social innovation and successful cooperativist actions. *International Journal of Quality and Service Sciences, 4*(4), 332–344.

FORUM. (2005). *Housing workshops: Knowing what people really want*, vol. 2. Housing Workshops Booklets. Retrieved November 20, 2013, from http://archief.forum.nl/woonateliers/index-engels.html

Fung, A., & Wright, E. O. (2001). Deepening democracy: Innovations in empowered participatory governance. *Politics & Society, 29*(1), 5–41.

Geddes, A. (2000). Lobbying for migrant inclusion in the European Union: New opportunities for transnational advocacy? *Journal of European Public Policy, 7*(4), 632–649.

Habermas, J. (1984). *The theory of communicative action. Volume I: Reason and the rationalisation of society*. Boston, MA: Beacon.

Harvard Joint Centre for Housing Studies. (2012). Joint Centre for Housing Studies of Harvard University. Retrieved November, 29, 2013, from http://www.jchs.harvard.edu/research/finance.html

Kettunen, J. (1997). Education and unemployment duration. *Economics of Education Review, 16*, 163–170.

Ministerio de Educación, Políticas Sociales y Deporte. (2008). *El plan de intervención social de los barrios de la Estrella y la Milagrosa de Albacete obtiene sus primeros resultados* [The plan for social intervention in *La Estrella* and *La Milagrosa* neighbourhoods in Albacete obtain its first results]. Retrieved November, 29, 2013, from http://sid.usal.es/mostrarficha.asp?id=13542&fichero=1.1

Mircea, T., & Dorobantu, D. (2008). *Impact of education in terms of housing opportunities—migrants and ethnic minorities. Interim report*. Universitatea de Vest Timisoara: INCLUD-ED Project, 6th Framework Programme, European Commission.

OECD. (2005). Recommendation principles and good practices for financial education and awareness. Retrieved November, 29, 2013, from http://www.oecd.org/finance/financial-education/35108560.pdf

Ottawa Charter for Health Promotion. (1986). *First International Conference on Health Promotion, Otawa, 21ˢᵗ of Novembre of 1986*. Retrieved November, 29, 2013, from http://www.paho.org/English/AD/SDE/HS/OttawaCharterEng.pdf

Padrós, M., García, R., Rodrigues de Mello, R., & Molina, S. (2011). Contrasting scientific knowledge with knowledge from the lifeworld: The dialogic inclusion contract. *Qualitative Inquiry, 17*(3), 304–312.

Pilgram, A., et al. (2001). *Social exclusion as a multidimensional process: Subcultural and formally assisted strategies of coping with and avoiding social exclusion*. Brussels: European Commission.

Puigvert, L., Christou, M., & Holdford, J. (2012). Critical communicative methodology: Including vulnerables voices in research through dialogue. *Cambridge Journal of Education, 42*(4), 513–526.

Rudd, R. E., Moeykens, B. A., & Colton, T. C. (1999). Health and literacy. A review of medical and public health literature. *Annual Review of Adult Learning and Literacy, 1*(5). Retrieved November, 20, 2013, from http://www.ncsall.net/index.html@id=522.html

Santa Cruz, I., Siles, G., & Vrecer, N. (2011). Invest for the long term or attend to immediate needs? Schools and the employment of less educated youths and adults. *European Journal of Education, 46*(2), 197–208.

Sen, A. (1999). *Development as freedom*. New York: Oxford University Press.

Social Exclusion Unit. (2001). *Preventing social exclusion. Report by the social exclusion unit*. London: Cabinet Office.

Stein, J. (1997). *Empowerment & women's health: Theory, methods and practice*. London: Zed books.

Territoriale Beschäftigungspakte in Österreich Zwischenbilanz. (2011). Herausgeberin: Koordinationsstelle der TEPs in Österreich am Zentrum für Soziale Innovation, im Auftrag des Bundesministeriums für Arbeit, Soziales und Konsumentenschutz.

Wolbers, M. (2000). The effects of level of education on mobility between employment and unemployment in the Netherlands. *European Sociological Review, 16*, 185–200.

Xu, G., Fields, S. K., Laine, C., Veloski, J. J., Barzansky, B., & Martini, C. J. (1997). The relationship between the race/ethnicity of generalist physicians and their care for underserved populations. *American Journal of Public Health, 87*(5), 817–822.

Zippel, K. (2004). Transnational advocacy networks and policy cycles in the European Union: The case of sexual harassment. *Social Politics, 11*(1), 57–85.

Chapter 8
Same Resources, Better Results: Recommendations for Educational Policy

Based on the data provided in the previous chapters, recommendations for educational policy should include the need to invest in evidence-based policies, as a way to improve results and reduce cost. This is particularly important in the midst of a worldwide economic recession. Some of these recommendations are: foster educational policies based on Successful Educational Actions; base teacher training on scientific evidence; encourage inclusive successful actions that eliminate both *streaming* and *mixture* practices; develop *interactive groups* in classrooms; facilitate *dialogic reading*; favor the *extension of learning time* without reducing curricular goals; foster family education in schools related to learning outcomes; enhance inclusive vocational training.

The study of schools across Europe and communities involved in educational projects that have shown progress in their educational results led to the identification of Successful Educational Actions (SEAs). Integrative Successful Actions (ISAs) involving other social areas—employment, housing, health and social and political participation—that promote inclusion in these areas by incorporating Successful Educational Actions have also been identified. The 5 years of scientific research concluded with an exhaustive, state-of-the-art understanding of education and its connection to other social areas, but most importantly, this experience has allowed us to define SEAs and ISAs.

INCLUD-ED has identified successful actions that address school failure: heterogeneous groupings achieved by reallocating existing human resources, *extended learning time*, and certain types of family and community education. These successful actions demonstrated the inaccuracy of discourses that tend to blame students or their environment for school failure, especially students with minority or immigrant backgrounds. On the contrary, we found that when these actions are implemented in predominantly immigrant and minority schools located in disadvantaged areas, their educational results improve. Therefore, the crucial factor is not the composition of the student body, but rather the type of educational action that is implemented. Successful types of participation by families and community members become a significant potential resource to improve educational and social inclusion. Five types of participation were identified: informative, consultative, evaluative (i.e., of the center and students), decisive (in decision-making, including

© The Author(s) 2015
R. Flecha (Ed.), INCLUD-ED Consortium, *Successful Educational Actions for Inclusion and Social Cohesion in Europe*, SpringerBriefs in Education,
DOI 10.1007/978-3-319-11176-6_8

academic aspects) and educative. The last three favor educational success to the greatest extent. Specifically, the data shed light on the importance of successful Family Education programs. Previous theories and research demonstrated that promoting cultural and educational interactions between students and social agents, and more particularly with family members, enhances student achievement. Certain family education and community engagement programs that promote these type of interactions have led students whose families have only a few books at home or limited academic qualifications to obtain excellent academic results. The *dialogic literary gatherings* are the best example of this type of successful family education. The data reveal that this family education program has substantial positive effects on the students' motivation and academic success.

Additionally, once successful actions have transformed the school, the process can be extended to the other areas of society (i.e., employment, housing, health, and political and social participation). The main finding consists in recreating the identified, research-based successful Integrative Actions by engaging in dialogue with the area's residents. The connection between processes of social exclusion and inclusion and educational opportunities from the social agent's perspective has been analyzed among five vulnerable groups, namely, migrants, women, cultural minorities, youth and persons with disabilities.

During the project, and by analyzing schools that were successfully improving their students' academic results, it has been possible to gather sufficient evidence that these actions can be recreated in any context and therefore support school success. Successful actions have been identified in different contexts across Europe, thereby highlighting what the studied schools had in common in particular respects (e.g., what type of relationship they established with families, student groupings, etc.). The SEAs identified by the project have already been transferred to other contexts, countries, and continents and have obtained excellent results, as they were not merely transposed but recreated in dialogue with the individuals living in those areas. Therefore, they are not successful, isolated experiences but successful actions that have universal components and can be transferred elsewhere. This makes it possible to overcome contextualist perspectives in education that have long legitimated inequalities and, potentially, to use successful actions as the basis for educational and social policy.

During the project, we demonstrated that the successful actions we identified could be recreated in particular contexts to respond to the specific demands of the population, complementing the universal dimension with contextual components. The Dialogic Inclusion Contract is a particular procedure found to serve to this purpose while including the voices of end-users as key actors in decision making, and it has also been identified as an effective component of actions promoting inclusion in different social areas. Overall, these findings constitute a scientific basis that can help to replace interventions based on non-scientific assumptions with those based on scientific evidence and transfer these positive results promoted by successful actions to additional contexts. Moving from assumptions to evidence in education by developing evidence-based policies makes it possible to achieve substantially better results with the same resources. The findings presented here are intended to enhance the educational and social inclusion of larger numbers of individuals, especially children and youths, who have been the leitmotiv of the project, informing policies that support achieving the European social cohesion objective established for the next decade.

Drawing from primary results of the project, INCLUD-ED has elaborated a list of policy recommendations, which can be discussed and developed at the EU and member state levels, as well as the regional and local levels.

8.1 Same Resources, Better Results: Successful Educational Actions to Transform European Schools

- *Foster educational policies based on Successful Educational Actions*, which have been scientifically demonstrated to both increase academic results and improve social cohesion in the school and beyond. Health policies are based on scientific evidence concerning the most successful treatments; we need educational policies based on scientific evidence regarding the most successful educational actions.
- *Base teacher trainingon scientific evidence.* Teacher training is crucial for ensuring the best educational results. Receiving this training allows teachers to know what works in education and become accustomed to seeking out scientific evidence on the most effective outcomes. This scientific teacher training enables them to move away from assumptions and base their work on evidence. It is advisable to provide in-service training in schools that are achieving the best results in relation to their socio-economic status.
- *Encourage inclusive successful actions that eliminate both streaming and mixture practices. Mixture* is the traditional way of organizing heterogeneous classrooms and does not guarantee that each of the pupils' needs receive attention. *Streaming* or ability grouping widens the achievement gap in academic performance and legitimizes the low attainment of some pupils. There are inclusion actions that have already demonstrated their success for children.
- *Promote educational actions that achieve better results with the same resources.* Research demonstrates that when existing human resources (often used to separate children into special groups or classrooms) are reorganized into inclusive successful actions, schools improve all pupils' academic achievement, including that of Roma and migrant pupils and children with disabilities. These successful actions include *interactive groups*, afterschool learning programs and *dialogic reading*.
- *Develop interactive groups in classrooms. Interactive groups* accelerate children's learning, increase academic achievement, and improve social relations. Pupils do not leave the regular classroom; instead, all supports are included in the classroom, and students are placed in small, heterogeneous groups with more adults in the classroom (teachers, educators, support or special education

teachers or social workers, relatives, siblings, community members or other volunteers). *Interactive groups* guarantee the success of all students.

- *Support extended learning time without reducing curricular goals.* Schools can extend students' learning time to implement Successful Educational Actions to foster children's attainment. This can also be accomplished by using existing human resources (professional or volunteer) in afterschool, weekend and holiday programs. Children who require additional support can receive it without being removed from the regular classroom or reducing curricular goals. Some successful examples are homework clubs, afterschool clubs, tutored libraries and weekend centers. These activities include learning core subjects, such as support for language learning, literacy or mathematics.

- *Facilitate dialogic reading: more persons, more time, and more spaces.* Reading is an action that occurs in many and diverse contexts at a variety of times (beyond school hours), in many spaces (from the classroom to the home and the street) and with numerous individuals (with peers, friends, family members, teachers, neighbors, volunteers and other community members). Children from all social backgrounds improve their communication skills and increase reading fluency when this approach is pursued.

- *Encourage decisive, evaluative and educative types of family and community participation.* Schools should develop mechanisms for the participation of family and community members, especially by vulnerable groups (migrants, cultural minorities, and students with disabilities). Research has demonstrated that these mechanisms have the greatest positive effect on pupils' success, in both academic and non-academic respects. In addition to participating in school decision-making processes (decisive) and the evaluation of children and the curriculum (evaluative), family and community members can participate in the children's learning process (educative). In this respect, educative participation in children's learning activities should focus on learning activities for core subjects, either activities during regular school hours or afterschool activities. Allowing and promoting family and community participation in these spaces entails taking advantage of the resources available in the community and making them available to respond to the pupils' learning needs, thereby increasing their learning opportunities.

- *Involve female relatives and other women from the community* in different school activities to help schools overcome gender inequalities, including gender violence. This is enabled through decisive and educative participation that enable overcoming gender prejudices. These forms of participation also enable family and community participation in deciding the school norms and sharing educative spaces where violent situations can be detected, prevented and eradicated from a coordinated communitarian action.

- *Foster family education in schools that is related to learning outcomes.* While some interpretations of statistics from international surveys argue that there is a relationship between parental education levels and children's learning outcomes, there is a need to break from the determinist prejudice that creates negative expectations for the families lacking academic backgrounds. Families' low educational levels only have a major influence when Successful Educational Actions are not implemented. Certain family education actions have demonstrated that we do not need to wait for the next (better prepared) generation to escape the vicious circle of educational inequality. Family education should respond to participants' educational needs, as they express them, to improve their educational levels to increase their opportunities to be integrated socially and in the labor market, better endowed to help their children to learn, or receive information on topics relevant to them. Among the successful actions in family education identified by INCLUD-ED are *dialogic literary gatherings*, host language learning and other activities focused on learning core subjects.

- *Dialogic literary gatherings are an example of a successful family education* in which individuals who had never read a book and, in general, those lacking an academic background, read and discuss classic works of world literature. These authors may include, among many others, Tolstoy, Shakespeare, Homer, Kafka, Sophocles, Cervantes, Zola, and Orwell. Through *dialogic literary gatherings*, family and community members improve their literacy and advance in a critical reading of social reality.
- *Support the development of schools as learning communities. Schools as learning communities* agree on a common vision and increase the commitment of pupils, parents, teachers and stakeholders to supporting school quality. They all focus on school improvement and take ownership of their own learning process through assisting with the implementation of Successful Educational Actions. Based on scientific evidence, this program of school transformation has been recommended by the European Commission and the European Council.[1]
- *Move forward beyond ghettoes in Europe through the Dialogic Inclusion Contract.* Through the Dialogic Inclusion Contract, teachers, social workers, families, administration, community organizations and researchers discuss evidence of successful actions provided in research. The objective is to recreate the successful actions for their context to overcome educational and social exclusion.
- *Facilitate Integrative Successful Actions.* The implementation of Successful Educational Actions in schools leads to social transformations in the same communities in other areas of society, such as employment, health, housing and political participation. Research shows that successful actions in these social areas, which contribute to social inclusion, include an educational component based on the SEAs.
- *Enhance inclusive vocational training*, which allows youth to return to the educational system and advance to higher education, contributing to avoiding unemployment. Instead of reducing vocational training to curriculums that only focus on specific skills for concrete occupations, inclusive vocational training

---

[1] European Commission. (2011). *Communication from the Commission to the European Parliament, the Council, the European Economic and Social Committee and the Committee of the Regions. Tackling Early School Leaving: a key contribution to the Europe 2020 agenda.* Brussels: European Commission.

includes academic subjects necessary to obtain higher qualifications, in conjunction with workplace-related skills. This guarantees that the youths in these programs study a more thorough and integrated curriculum. Therefore, they acquire both the key competences for lifelong learning that they will need in the labor market and maintain the possibility of accessing academic tracks that can lead to higher education and better working conditions in the long term.

Index

A
Academic achievement, 13, 28, 47, 48, 73, 101
Academic success, 1, 6, 16, 31, 34, 47, 48, 56, 100
After-school
   writing club, 38
Apple, Michael, 69, 71

B
Beane, James, 69
Best practices, 1, 3, 4
Bruner, Jerome, 10

C
Classroom arrangement
   inclusion, 6, 21, 23, 25, 32, 36, 51
   mixture, 6, 21, 22, 99, 101
   streaming, 6, 21–24, 26
Close referents, 90
Coexistence, 47, 51, 57, 59, 71, 73, 86
Committee
   advisory, 11
   management, 73
   mixed, 56, 57, 72, 73
Communicative
   methodology, 5, 9–11
   perspective, 9–11
   research, 9–12, 18
Communities, 1, *see also* learning
   communities
Community involvement, 16, 47, 48, 62, 67–69, 70
Cooperative
   Mondragon Cooperative Corporation, 81
   worker-owned cooperative, 94
Council of Europe, 6, 9, 67

CREA, 5, 71, 75
Curriculum, 18, 21–24, 32, 33, 37, 41, 54, 59, 60, 69, 71, 80, 102–104

D
Decision making, 72, 79, 81, 82, 85, 87, 88, 93, 99, 100, 102
Dialogue
   egalitarian, 53, 70, 85, 93
   evaluation, 6, 60
   inclusion contract, 7, 79, 80, 87, 92, 93, 100, 103
   intersubjective, 6, 10
   learning, 26, 71
   literary gatherings, 6, 18, 41–43, 47, 49, 53, 54, 100, 103, *see also* Dialogic reading
   reading, 6, 31, 39, 41, 42, 47, 53, 92, 99, 101, 102
   report, 60
Dimensions
   exclusionary, 12
   transformative, 12

E
Early school leaving, 4, 6, 12, 13, 18, 67, 70, 73, 74
Educational
   practices and systems, 3
   reforms, 3, 13, 21, 23
   success, 1, 2, 4, 21, 24, 26, 28, 31, 43, 44, 47, 55, 70, 71, 79, 83, 92, 99–103
   systems, 3, 21, 26, 47
Effective networking, 84
Efficiency and equity, 26

© The Author(s) 2015
R. Flecha (Ed.), INCLUD-ED Consortium, *Successful Educational Actions for Inclusion and Social Cohesion in Europe*, SpringerBriefs in Education,
DOI 10.1007/978-3-319-11176-6

108 Index

Printing: Ten Brink, Meppel, The Netherlands
Binding: Ten Brink, Meppel, The Netherlands